SEA HARRIER FRS 1
VS
MIRAGE III/DAGGER
South Atlantic 1982

DOUGLAS C. DILDY AND PABLO CALCATERRA

OSPREY PUBLISHING
Bloomsbury Publishing Plc

Kemp House, Chawley Park, Cumnor Hill, Oxford OX2 9PH, UK
29 Earlsfort Terrace, Dublin 2, Ireland
1385 Broadway, 5th Floor, New York, NY 10018, USA
Email: info@ospreypublishing.com
www.ospreypublishing.com

OSPREY is a trademark of Osprey Publishing Ltd

First published in Great Britain in 2017

A catalogue record for this book is available from the British Library.

Print ISBN: 978 1 4728 1889 8
ePub: 978 1 4728 1891 1
ePDF: 978 1 4728 1890 4
XML: 978 1 4728 2191 1

Edited by Tony Holmes
Cover artwork and battlescene by Gareth Hector
Three-views, cockpits, armament scrap views and Engaging the Enemy
artwork by Jim Laurier
Maps and formation diagrams by www.bounford.com
Index by Fionbar Lyons
Typeset in ITC Conduit and Adobe Garamond
Page layouts by PDQ Digital Media Solutions, Bungay, UK
Printed and bound in India by Replika Press Private Ltd.

22 23 24 25 26   10 9 8 7 6 5 4 3

The Woodland Trust
Osprey Publishing supports the Woodland Trust, the UK's leading
woodland conservation charity.

www.ospreypublishing.com
To find out more about our authors and books visit our website. Here you
will find extracts, author interviews, details of forthcoming events and the
option to sign-up for our newsletter.

Sea Harrier FRS 1 Cover Art

Mid-afternoon on 1 May 1982 – the first and only day of combat between
Royal Navy Sea Harrier FRS 1s and *Fuerza Aérea Argentina* Mirage
IIIEAs – two SHARs, led by Flt Lt Paul Barton, performed a near-perfect
'hook' attack against a pair of Mirage interceptors. While Barton's wingman,
Lt Steve Thomas, intercepted the Mirages head-on, Barton offset low and to
the north, curving in behind the Mirages just as the wingman, 1Lt Carlos
Perona, began a vertical scissors manoeuvre against Thomas. As Barton pulled
the SHAR's nose around to point his AIM-9L at Perona's afterburner, he was
greeted by the tell-tale sound of seeker-head 'acquisition' growling in his
headset, and fired the missile. Barton later recalled, 'At first I thought it had
failed. It came off the rail and ducked down. It took about half-a-mile for it to
get its trajectory sorted out, then it picked itself up and for the last half-mile
just homed straight in. The missile flight time was about four seconds, and
then the missile hit him on the port side of the fuselage, then the whole rear
half of the aircraft disappeared in a great ball of flame. The front half went
down burning fiercely, arcing [downwards] towards the sea.' (Artwork by
Gareth Hector)

Dagger Cover Art

When, on the morning of 21 May 1982, the Argentine air command was
alerted that the Royal Navy's 12-ship amphibious task group had begun
unloading troops and equipment in San Carlos Sound, a major air strike –
12 Daggers and 12 Skyhawks, with four Mirage IIIEAs flying top cover – was
ordered off to attack them. Sea Harriers orbiting in over-water CAPs were only
able to intercept and shoot down two A-4Cs. Meanwhile, the Daggers got
through to hit the destroyer HMS *Antrim* with a bomb and strafed two
frigates. This prompted the SHARs to move their CAPs over West Falkland/
Gran Malvinas to be better positioned to intercept the afternoon wave of
attacks. At about 1500hrs, the 801 NAS CAP, manned by Lt Cdr Nigel
'Sharkey' Ward and Lt Steve Thomas, spotted two of the three Daggers of
Ratón Flight and immediately engaged, with Thomas shooting down both in
quick succession. Flying the third Dagger, Capt Gustavo Piuma Justo saw the
second SHAR (Ward) ahead of him gently turning to the right at around
120ft above the ground. Piuma descended and manoeuvred inside Ward's turn
and, beginning at approximately 2,000ft range, he fired a long burst at the
SHAR. Without tracers, it was impossible to aim accurately. Consequently, his
cannon fire failed to hit the aircraft. Ward flew into a valley slightly off to the
right and Piuma thought he could catch him by heading down the left side of
the hill. While flying at 450 knots and 130ft above the ground, he saw a pilot
hanging from his parachute (Ratón 2; Lt Jorge Senn). Shortly thereafter,
Piuma's jet shuddered as a result of a great explosion, and he ejected when he
felt the heat of the fire raging behind his cockpit. Distracted by the parachute,
Piuma had inadvertently flown ahead of Ward, who emerged from the valley
and spotted the Dagger, manoeuvred behind it and fired an AIM-9L.
(Artwork by Gareth Hector)

Note

In this book linear, weight and volume measurements are given in imperial
units of measurement: nautical miles, yards, feet, inches, long tons and
pounds. There are exceptions, such as weapons calibre, where metric is used in
some cases, depending on the context. The following data will help when
converting between imperial and metric measurements:

1 nautical mile (nm) = 1.85km
1 yard = 91.44cm
1ft = 30.48cm
1in = 2.54cm
Mach 1 = 666.75 knots
1 knot = 1.85km/h
1 ton = 2,240lb/1.016 tonnes
1lb = 0.454kg

Because of the close similarity between radar (6,080ft) and nautical miles
(6,076ft), Western radars use nautical miles for range information, which also
makes it compatible with airspeed and navigation information used in flight.
All distance references in this work are in nautical miles. A nautical mile is
1.1508 statute miles.

CONTENTS

INTRODUCTION

The Falklands/Malvinas War was one of the most unlikely conflicts in modern history, its origins being exceedingly complex, inflammably contentious and vociferously debated by both sides proceeding and throughout the war – they remain so even today.

Originally settled by the French in 1764 and the British one year later (although initially each was unaware of the other's presence), the Falkland Islands/Islas Malvinas were acquired by Spain from France in 1766. The Spanish forced the British to abandon their settlement four years later. The islands were then incorporated as part of the Viceroyalty of the Río de la Plata and ceded to the United Provinces of the Río de la Plata – later renamed Argentina – after it won its independence in 1816. A permanent Argentine population was established in 1823, but ten years later the settlers were forcibly removed by Britain. Despite Argentina's diplomatic protests, Queen Victoria incorporated the islands into the British Empire as a Crown colony in 1843.

While both sides remained intensely adamant about their national sovereignty over the disputed islands, the issue devolved into a matter of possession, and since 1833 the islands have been possessed by – and populated by – the British. In 1965 UN Resolution 2065 recognised the disputed nature of the islands' sovereignty and determined that bilateral negotiations should be undertaken to resolve the issue. These were ongoing when the British Ministry of Defence (MoD) issued its 1981 Defence White Paper proposing large-scale naval cuts, including decommissioning the locally based icebreaker/patrol ship HMS *Endurance* and withdrawing the Royal Marines detachment from the islands. To Argentina's ruling *Junta* it appeared that the British government no longer intended to retain possession of the islands. Consequently, in order to strengthen its negotiating position in the sovereignty dispute talks, the *Junta* forcibly repossessed the islands on 2 April 1982, precipitating the otherwise completely unlikely conflict between the waning imperial nation and the local regional power.

The resulting war also pitted two unlikely adversaries in air-to-air combat. Developed as a French supersonic interceptor in the 1950s, the *Fuerza Aérea Argentina's* (FAA) Dassault Mirage IIIEA and its subsequent air-to-ground derivative of the Mirage 5J, called the Dagger, assembled by Israeli Aircraft Industries (IAI), were confronted by the Royal Navy's relatively limited, decidedly subsonic V/STOL (vertical/short take-off and landing) fleet air defence fighter, the British Aerospace (BAe) Sea Harrier Fighter, Reconnaissance, Strike (FRS) Mk 1, commonly called the 'SHAR'. The latter, developed in the 1970s from the Royal Air Force's ground-hugging BAe Harrier GR 3 army-supporting light attack aircraft, was technologically more advanced than the Mirage variants, but was not designed to operate in the same flight envelope (defined chiefly by altitude and air speeds) as its Argentine adversaries. Therefore, pilots of both types were forced to modify their doctrine, roles and tactics significantly to meet the challenges and the threat posed by the other. Aside from – and certainly in no way discounting – the skill, determination, courage and sacrifice demonstrated by the pilots of both sides, it is their adaptation of their tactics, and flying their aircraft in ways that were unforeseen prior to the conflict, that make the study of the 'duel' between the Sea Harrier FRS 1 and the Mirage IIIEA/Dagger so engagingly interesting.

ACKNOWLEDGEMENTS

Any attempt to reconstruct and describe accurately and objectively the aerial engagements in a war fought 35 years ago requires the contribution of numerous individuals, many of whom participated in the events described. Foremost, the authors thank the veterans from both sides of this otherwise unlikely war, not only for their selfless service to their respective nations and their efforts and sacrifice during that conflict, but also for their generous and considerate contributions to this book. From the Argentine side, the authors thank especially *Veterano de Guerra de Malvinas – Retirado* (Retired Malvinas War Veterans or VGM-R) Brigadier Mayor Guillermo Donadille and also Brigadiers Gustavo Piuma Justo and Carlos Perona, and Comodoros Raúl Díaz, Jorge Senn and Luis Puga for their combat accounts. From the British side, the authors are indebted to Retired Royal Navy Cdr Nigel 'Sharkey' Ward and Lt Cdrs Mike 'Soapy' Watson and David Smith for their selfless contributions.

While many books have addressed the Royal Navy's SHAR operations during this conflict, the ground work for this comparative study was laid by noted aviation historian Santiago Rivas through his comprehensive collection of pilot/participant interviews contained in his excellent *Wings of the Malvinas – The Argentine Air War over the Falklands* (Hikoki Publications, 2012), and we greatly appreciate his permission to use portions of them. We are also indebted to 'Sharkey' Ward for his permission to use excerpts from his first-hand account, *Sea Harrier over the Falklands – A Maverick at War* (Leo Cooper, 1992), to tell the story from the British perspective, as well as to 'Soapy' Watson for his incomparable assistance in getting the technical details and other aspects of flying the SHAR as close to correct as memory allows.

In addition to those mentioned above, the authors are also grateful to author, photographer and *Combat Aircraft* editor Jamie Hunter and *Aviation Classics* editor Tim Callaway for their provision of many of the photographs contained in this book. A Falklands war veteran, Tim was especially helpful in obtaining BAe Systems and Dassault Aviation SA images, as well as donating photographs from his own collection. The authors also thank Gabriel Fioni of the *Museo Nacional de Malvinas de Olivia* for his support with photographs from the museum archives, as well as Comodoro (VGM-R) Oscar Aranda Durañona and Eduardo Amores Olivier of the *Dirección de Estudios Históricos Fuerza Aérea Argentina*, and Comodoros (Ret) Nelson Godoy and Claudio Marcos of FAA Communications. In addition, we thank Vicecomodoro (VGM-R) Pablo M. R. Carballo, Luis Litrenta and Mayor (VGM-R) Guillermo Posadas and Juan Manuel Mothe for their images.

Finally, we also thank Falkland Islands resident Allan White for his great work in aviation archaeology and crash investigation, solving the mystery and correcting the historical record concerning the loss of Capt García Cuerva and Mirage IIIEA I-015.

PUBLISHER'S NOTE

In this book the naming of the Falkland Islands – known to Argentina as Islas Malvinas – is derived from the official United Nations (UN) convention of appending the name 'Falklands' with 'Malvinas' in brackets. Herein, the co-authors have provided an objective and forthright account, telling both sides of the story of the air battles fought between the opposing pilots flying Sea Harriers and Mirage/Daggers and, in deference to our Argentine co-author and contributors, Osprey has accepted the UN convention, but for readability purposes has chosen to render the naming as 'Falklands/Malvinas' instead of 'Falklands [Malvinas]'. While, like the UN convention, this arrangement acknowledges the continuing sovereignty dispute between the UK and Argentine claims to the islands, it should not be construed as the publisher's recognition of the Argentine claim. For ready reference, an English/Spanish place-names glossary is provided at the end of the book.

Designed to counter large, high-flying Soviet maritime reconnaissance platforms such as the Tupolev Tu-95 'Bear-D', these factory-fresh Sea Harrier FRS 1s of 800 NAS were embarked in HMS *Invincible* for its 'work ups' in 1980.

CHRONOLOGY

1953   *Armée de l'Air* solicits design proposals for high altitude Mach 2 bomber interceptor.

1955
25 June   First flight of Dassault MD 550 Mystère Delta prototype.

1956
5 May   Extensively modified following initial flight testing, the MD 550 – now renamed the Mirage I – demonstrates significantly improved performance.

17 November   First flight of Dassault Mirage III prototype.

1960
9 October   First flight of Mirage IIIC interceptor.

1961
13 March   First flight of the Hawker Siddeley P.1127 VTOL (vertical take-off and landing) experimental prototype.

5 April   First flight of the improved multi-role Mirage IIIE.

7 July   First Mirage IIIC is delivered to *Armée de l'Air* – three months later, Israel orders its third batch of 24 Mirage IIICJs.

1963
8 February   P.1127 XP831 lands on board HMS *Ark Royal*.

1964
7 March   First flight of the Hawker Siddeley Kestrel FGA 1.

The diminutive MD 550 Mystère Delta was designed as a 'lightweight' point-defence interceptor. The progenitor of the entire line of Dassault delta-winged Mirages, its first flight was on 25 June 1955. (© Dassault Aviation)

1965

15 December   UN Resolution 2065 calls on the governments of Argentina and UK to negotiate 'with a view to finding a peaceful solution' to the sovereignty dispute over the Falkland Islands/Islas Malvinas. Negotiations proceed in a desultory fashion for the next 12 years.

1966

31 August   First flight of the Hawker Siddeley Harrier developmental aircraft.

1967

19 May   First flight of the dedicated ground attack variant of the Mirage III, designated the Mirage 5J.

5–10 June   Arab–Israeli Six Day War – Israeli Defence Force/Air Force (IDF/AF) Mirage IIICJs claim destruction of 50.5 enemy aircraft, for the loss of nine.

1969

1 January   First Royal Air Force (RAF) Harrier GR 1 unit – No. 1(F) Sqn – declared operational.

1970

October   Argentina orders its first ten – of an eventual 17 – Mirage IIIEA interceptors.

1971

21 March   First flight of the IAI-assembled Nesher S single-seat ground attack variant of the Mirage III.

1973

July   FAA activates the *I Escuadrón de Caza Interceptora* (1st Fighter Interceptor Squadron) with the Mirage IIIEA. Unit expanded into *Grupo 8 de Caza* in December 1975.

1975

15 May   MoD announces order for 24 Sea Harrier FRS Mk 1s, later increased to 34.

1978

20 August   Maiden flight of first production Sea Harrier FRS 1 XZ450.

December   Argentina purchases its first 24 – of an eventual 35 – Nesher Ss along with two (of eventual four) Nesher Ts from Israel as Dagger As and Bs.

1980

31 March   First operational Sea Harrier squadron – 800 Naval Air Squadron (NAS) – and the SHAR 'headquarters and training squadron' – 899 NAS – formed at RNAS Yeovilton.

1981

28 January   Second Sea Harrier squadron – 801 NAS – formed for deployment on board HMS *Invincible*.

29 March   The *Junta* of Army Commander-in-Chief General Leopoldo Galtieri, Navy commander Admiral Jorge Anaya and Air Force chief Brigadier General Basilio Dozo takes power in Argentina. Repossession of the Islas Malvinas becomes a national priority.

25 June   British government publishes MoD's 1981 Defence White Paper 'The UK Defence Programme – The Way Forward', inadvertently encouraging the *Junta* to consider repossessing the Falkland Islands/Islas Malvinas.

1982

18/19 March   While salvaging scrap-metal from abandoned whaling stations on South Georgia Island, Argentine workers raise their national flag over their camp, precipitating the British–Argentine confrontation over the possession of the Falkland Islands/Islas Malvinas and South Georgia Islands. Both respond by despatching naval auxiliaries and marines to South Georgia Island.

26 March   Argentina's *Junta* decide to forcibly repossess the Falkland Islands/Islas Malvinas, launching Operación *Rosario*.

2 April	Operación *Rosario* repossesses the islands for Argentina.	**14 June**	Argentine garrison at Port Stanley/ Puerto Argentino surrenders to British forces.
5 April	The Thatcher government responds by despatching a carrier and amphibious task force to the South Atlantic, beginning Operation *Corporate*.	**20 June**	British government announces that South Atlantic hostilities are concluded.
1 May	Negotiations fail to conclude the crisis peacefully. Combat operations over the islands begin with the 'Black Buck' (RAF Vulcan) and Sea Harrier bombing raids. First engagements between SHARs and Mirages/Daggers result in two Sea Harrier victories.		
21–25 May	Royal Navy amphibious task group (TG 317.0) arrives in San Carlos Water and begins disembarking troops for the land campaign. The Argentine response is a five-day long maritime air campaign using Dagger and Skyhawk fighter-bombers. Losses are high on both sides.		
8 June	Last Argentine anti-ship strike against Royal Navy amphibious operations.		

A completely unique naval combat aircraft of the 20th Century, Sea Harrier FRS 1 developmental airframe XZ440 performs a vertical landing at RNAS Yeovilton in April 1982. (Paul Crickmore)

DESIGN AND DEVELOPMENT

MIRAGE IIIEA

The Mirage IIIE was created as France's second-generation jet fighter, specifically designed as a supersonic bomber interceptor. During the post-World War II resurrection of the French aviation industry, Marcel Bloch returned from the infamous Nazi concentration camp at Buchenwald, in Germany, and re-established his company, taking a form of his late brother's wartime code-name – 'Char d'Assault' (literally 'assault vehicle', the French army term for 'battle tank'), which became 'Dassault' – as both his own surname and the name of his new enterprise, Société des Avions Marcel Dassault.

Beginning in 1947, Marcel Dassault started designing and producing a series of first-generation jet fighters for the *Armée de l'Air*. These were the rather rotund, straight-wing MD 450 Ouragan ('Hurricane', first flown in 1949), the sleeker, faster, swept-wing MD 452/454 Mystère II and IV (flown in 1951/52) and the transonic Super Mystère (1955). The last mentioned – very similar in almost all regards to the USAF North American Aviation F-100 Super Sabre – became the *Armée de l'Air* standard fighter-bomber for the next 20 years. Ouragans, Mystère IVs and Super Mystères were subsequently exported to Israel, which quickly became Dassault's favourite overseas customer.

With the Cold War intensifying and jet-powered nuclear bombers becoming the ultimate threat, in 1953 the *Armée de l'Air* canvassed France's reborn aviation industry for a high-altitude, Mach 2 interceptor. Specifically, the *Armée de l'Air* required a lightweight, high performance interceptor to be able to operate from short airstrips and reach Mach 2 and 18,000m (59,055ft) in under six minutes while carrying a single 200kg (440lb) air-to-air missile (AAM). Taking advantage of captured German technological research studies, principally by Walter Lippisch and the Horton brothers, three of the four responses were delta-wing designs, of which Dassault's MD 550 appeared most promising. Initially named the Mystère Delta, the design was to be powered by a pair of Turboméca Gabizo

afterburning turbojets and a detachable Société d'Etudes pour la Propulsion par Réaction (SEPR) liquid-fuel rocket motor. Issued on 22 March 1954, the *Armée de l'Air*'s contract called for the design, development and construction of two prototypes.

Because the Turboméca engines were not yet available, the first example of the diminutive, radar-less interceptor was powered by two licence-built non-afterburning 1,753lb thrust Armstrong Siddeley MD 30 Viper turbojets, augmented by a 3,300lb thrust SEPR 66 rocket mounted in a pod beneath the empennage. The MD 550's first flight was on the morning of 25 June 1955, with a second following that afternoon. Although handling proved to be acceptable, the prototype's performance – particularly its speed – was found wanting, so after six months of testing, it was returned to the factory for changes to be made to its rear fuselage, vertical fin and air intakes. All were made in an attempt to reduce drag and increase maximum speed.

Renamed the Mirage I due to the extensive redesign, the prototype returned to the air in May the following year and attained Mach 1.3 in level flight at high altitude while in full afterburner. It could also momentarily reach Mach 1.6 with the 20-second rocket motor boost from the SEPR 66. However, its traditional fuselage design, fixed inlets and low engine thrust precluded it from ever attaining the *Armée de l'Air* specification. Meanwhile, air force planners had realised that a visually aimed, radio-guided AAM placed unacceptable limitations on the weapon system. Consequently, the second prototype – the Mirage II, which was to be powered by 3,310lb thrust Gabizo turbojets and *two* SEPR rocket motors – was cancelled and the *Armée de l'Air* revised the specification for a larger, heavier, radar-equipped interceptor.

In the meantime, Dassault engineers had learned much from the Mirage I's delta wing and this, coupled with British flight test results from the Fairey Delta FD 2 experimental aircraft, resulted in the revised design having an entirely new, more sharply swept, and far more sophisticated wingform. Additionally, the introduction of the 'area rule' feature –

The disappointingly subsonic Mystère Delta was rebuilt as the Mirage I, but it was still considered too small – and too slow – to meet the *Armée de l'Air*'s interceptor requirement. However, as a supersonic test vehicle, it provided much useful data and experience. (© Dassault Aviation)

The resulting redesign – and second test article, the Mirage III – incorporated numerous features emerging from ongoing advances in supersonic flight technologies. Among these were the need for 'intake shock cones' to control the airflow to the engine face. (© Dassault Aviation)

Mirage IIIC No. 91 in flight, carrying a Matra R 530 IR missile and two RPK100 500-litre (110 gal) 'supersonique' external fuel tanks. The famous *Escadron de Chasse* (EC) 1/2 'Cigognes' ('Storks') was the first *Armée de l'Air* unit to become operational on the new Mach 2 interceptor, receiving its first example on 7 July 1961. (Author Collection)

whereby the fuselage cross-section is reduced to compensate for the increased area of the wings – assured the design of attaining higher Mach speeds. Finally, the switch to a single, vastly more powerful Société Nationale d'Etude et de Construction de Moteurs d'Aviation (SNECMA) development of Germany's wartime BMW 003 axial-flow turbojet provided the thrust needed. The much larger and longer engine also increased the aircraft's length, resulting in a more elegant design, increasing the 'fineness ratio' and contributing to higher speeds. Called the Atar – standing for Atelier Technique Aéronautique Rickenbach (after the SNECMA-funded technical centre in the French occupation zone of West Germany) – the seventh iteration of the engine, designated the 101G, produced 10,365lb of thrust in afterburner and became the powerplant for the successful Super Mystère fighter-bomber.

Because the larger, more powerful engine required greater volumes of air, and higher Mach necessitated active control of dynamic shock wave effects, the air intakes were again redesigned, moving them aft along the fuselage sides to allow increased 'capture volume' within the 'area rule' concept and incorporating movable F-104-style 'shock cones' to ensure the front of the SNECMA Atar turbojet received subsonic airflow. The combined result of these compound changes was the completely redesigned delta-winged interceptor known as the Mirage III, which completed its maiden flight on 17 November 1956.

Following extensive testing of ten Mirage IIIA pre-production examples – the variant's prototype becoming the first Western European-designed/built aircraft to achieve Mach 2 on 24 October, 1958 – the *Armée de l'Air* received its first operational Mirage IIIC interceptor in July 1961. Almost simultaneously the IDF/AF received its first 24 Mirage IIICJs, of an eventual 72 (including two Mirage IIICRJ reconnaissance variants), augmented by three Mirage IIIBJ two-seat combat trainers. The IDF/AF Mirage IIICJs' outstanding performance in the June 1967 Six Day War against Egypt and Syria – being credited with 50.5 victories while suffering only nine losses – proved the type's effectiveness as an air superiority fighter, elicited worldwide interest in the type and spurred further development.

While the Mirage IIIC had excellent speed and rate of climb, it was handicapped by limited range on internal fuel and unreliable avionics, especially its Compagnie Générale de Télégraphie Sans Fil (CSF) Cyrano Ibis air intercept (AI) radar. Dassault began developing a 'stretched version' – incorporating a 11.8in fuselage 'plug' immediately behind the cockpit – to provide increased fuel tankage and additional avionics components associated with the improved Cyrano II AI radar and the CSF/ Marconi analogue navigation computer, which was coupled with Marconi Doppler navigation radar mounted under the nose. Additionally, to help overcome its range limitations, the upgraded version was powered by the more fuel-efficient 13,668lb thrust Atar 09C-3 turbojet, which had an improved afterburner nozzle mechanism. With these upgrades came increased capabilities, allowing the new, longer-ranged variant – the Mirage IIIE – to also perform low-level ground attack missions and to deliver the AN 52 15-kiloton tactical nuclear weapon. Dassault's new multi-role fighter first flew on 5 April 1961, entering *Armée de l'Air* service three years later.

DAGGER

Very impressed with its Mirage IIICJs, the IDF/AF started looking for a newer and more effective type to replace its two squadrons of ageing Mystère IVs in the ground attack role in the early 1960s. Since aerial combat in the Middle East was primarily day, clear air fighting, the sophisticated avionics of the Mirage IIIE were superfluous, but its excellent performance would be improved by a lighter design. Consequently, in July 1965, the Israelis enquired if a modified version – minus the heavy Cyrano radar but with increased fuel tankage and weapons carriage capabilities – could be produced that would be cheaper to purchase and maintain, and that would be able to 'turn around' quickly between sorties.

The resulting study showed that removing the avionics and Doppler and AI radars (replacing the latter with a simple range-only system) reduced the weight by almost 1,000lb and allowed the internal fuel capacity to be increased by 32 per cent. Two extra pylons were also added to increase the combat payload to 4,000kg (8,820lb), while the under-wing missile stations were retained, permitting the carrying of AIM-9 Sidewinder or Mécanique Aviation Traction (or Matra) R 550 Magic infra-red (IR) 'heat-seeking' missiles for self-protection and a secondary air-to-air capability.

Before the specialised ground-attack prototype – called the Mirage 5J ('J' for 'Juif', 'Jewish' in French) – even flew, on 7 April 1966, the Israeli government contracted with Dassault for the delivery of 50 examples of the new variant, plus two Mirage 5DJ combat trainers. The following year, and prior to their delivery, President Charles de Gaulle unilaterally imposed a government embargo on the sale of 'offensive arms' to the warring nations in the Middle East (the ban was primarily directed at Israel). The 50 idle attack aircraft were finally acquired by the *Armée de l'Air* as Mirage 5Fs in October 1971.

Embargoed Mirage 5Js in storage at Châteaudun AB. In October 1971 the 50 'Israeli jets' were purchased by the French government to equip ECs' 3/3 'Ardennes', 2/13 'Alpes' and 3/13 'Auvergne'. (Author Collection)

DAGGER A

51ft 0.5in

13ft 11.5in

C-403

26ft 11.5in

Needing to replace losses from the Six Day War, as well as supplant its obsolescent Mystère IVs, the IDF/AF quickly negotiated the purchase of 48 new Douglas A-4H Skyhawks while it engaged in heated discussions with Avions Dassault to obtain the company's assistance in creating a

substitute for the sequestered Mirage 5Js. With Dassault's founder and president being a Jew who had personally experienced the Holocaust, there was little popular support for de Gaulle's embargo, especially after the French government violated its own policy by selling 100 Mirage III/5s to Libya. According to an IAI engineer, 'The opponents [of the embargo] sought, and found, a way of aiding Israel'.

Dassault rationalised that, since it was a private company, the government embargo did not apply to it, so in January 1968 a manufacturing licence was sold to a consortium consisting of IAI and the North American Rockwell Corporation. As part of the agreement, Dassault secretly 'supplied specialised jigs, fixtures and tooling, as well as a substantial variety of large airframe components', including (reportedly) two completed airframes that were used as manufacturing examples and are referred to as Nesher 'prototypes'. The airframe components provided by Dassault included complete forward fuselages built by Aérospatiale (a Dassault sub-contractor), as evidenced by the Aérospatiale manufacturer's data plates found affixed in Dagger cockpits in the FAA's 'boneyard'. To complete the subterfuge, 61 newly built Mirage 5J/5DJs – 59 in 'knocked-down kit form' – were sent to Aérospatiale, which shipped them (aboard USAF C-5A transports) to Israel, where they were assembled by IAI with the help of Rockwell engineers.

What Dassault could not supply was the Atar 9C turbojet engine. This was because SNECMA – which was contracted by Israel in February 1968 to provide technical data and support for the Atar 9C – was a French government-owned company and it had to comply with the embargo. However, 'where there's a will there's a way', and the Israeli government's newly established Bet-Shemesh Engines Ltd (founded in May 1968 as a joint venture by Turboméca and the State of Israel) sought an alternate means to provide the IDF/AF with depot-level maintenance for its Atar turbojets. For $250,000 Israeli agents obtained more than 200,000 blueprints and technical documents from an employee of the Swiss-based Sulzer Company, which built the Atar 9C under licence for Switzerland's *Flugwaffe*. With these documents as technical guidelines, and a large number of spare Atars on hand due to the replacement of the Mirage IIICJ by US-supplied McDonnell Douglas F-4E Phantom IIs, Bet-Shemesh was able to provide enough engines to power the 51 IAI-assembled single-seaters and ten two-seat trainers, which more than replaced the 50 embargoed Mirage 5Js.

Named the Nesher ('Vulture'), the Israeli variant was 'almost an exact duplicate of the Mirage 5J, differing mainly in the installation of a Martin-Baker [Mk 6] ejector seat and locally sourced electronics'. The first example was flown on 21 March 1971

To replace the 50 embargoed Mirage 5Js, IAI assembled 51 sets of airframe sub-assemblies provided by Aérospatiale and called them Neshers. Nesher 526 (S-26) was used to score two victories against Egyptian aircraft. (Andreas Klein Collection)

OPPOSITE
Dagger C-403 was flown by Capt Guillermo Donadille during his engagements on 1 and 21 May 1982. Donadille was one of the only three Dagger pilots to shoot at a Sea Harrier during the conflict. Having started its life as Nesher S-16, it was delivered to Argentina in late 1978. This aircraft was shot down on 21 May by an AIM-9L fired by Lt Steve Thomas after Donadille engaged Lt Cdr Nigel 'Sharkey' Ward with his Dagger's 30mm guns at extremely low altitude and 450 knots above West Falkland/ Gran Malvina. Note that during the conflict FAA Daggers typically flew in either the air-to-air (Shafrir-2) or air-to-ground (bombs) configuration.

and the first unit was operational seven months later. The aircraft's combat debut came two years later in the October 1973 Yom Kippur War, its pilots claiming 115 victories during that conflict and afterwards. Following IAI's development of a much-modified and improved version of the Mirage 5J airframe powered by a licence-built General Electric J79 – known as the Kfir ('Young Lion') – the IDF/AF's less-capable Neshers soon became excess to its needs and, in 1978, were sold to Argentina as Daggers.

SEA HARRIER FRS 1

By the time the Neshers were fighting the Yom Kippur War, in a different military venue entirely, the Royal Navy was on the search for a new fleet air defence fighter. Downsizing as it relinquished its worldwide commitments to concentrate on protecting NATO's vital North Atlantic sea lanes, the Royal Navy's carrier force at this time had been reduced to the surviving icon of British naval aviation, the 36,800-ton (standard load) HMS *Ark Royal*, and two 18,300-ton anti-submarine warfare (ASW) helicopter carriers, HMS *Bulwark* and HMS *Hermes*. Originally, these were due to be replaced by a modern 50,000-ton attack carrier ('CVA-01') and two supporting 16,000-ton ASW 'through-deck cruisers' (HMS *Invincible* and HMS *Illustrious*), but CVA-01 was cancelled in 1966 and the 18-year-old *Ark Royal* was slated for retirement in the mid-1970s. This left the even older ASW carriers and lighter cruisers – none of which were capable of operating modern, conventional fixed-wing carrier aircraft – to carry on the Fleet Air Arm's traditional fleet air defence duties. What was needed was a proper multi-role fighter that would not require the usual assortment of heavy steam catapults and arresting cables associated with the operation of traditional carrier aircraft.

The first Hawker Siddeley P.1127 prototype, XP831, making a transition from vertical to forward flight in September 1961.

Fortunately, in yet another completely different military venue, developing V/STOL technologies had brought the Harrier light attack jet to operational status. Its adaptation to maritime roles was both obvious and timely. The genus of this unique capability began in 1956 with the confluence of events and the technological development of the Bristol Engines ducted turbofan (designated BE 52) and Hawker Siddeley's V/STOL experimental proof-of-concept aircraft designated the P.1127. Subsidised by NATO's Mutual Weapons Development Programme office, the team headed by legendary designer Sir Sidney Camm drew out the contours of a slim, sleek, single-seat light attack aircraft built around the BE 53/2 (later called the 'Pegasus 2') engine and its four rotatable exhaust nozzles.

The project was boosted, in March 1959, by the national General Operational Requirement 345 which expressed the RAF need for a V/STOL ground attack jet that could 'disperse and operate . . . in the field' in the event that Warsaw Pact tactical nuclear weapons rendered traditional RAF Germany airfields unusable.

The June 1960 contract resulted in six prototypes being built, the first (XP831) hovering (tethered) in October that year, with its first flight being on 13 March 1961. During the test programme two were lost, but great advances were made in the vectored thrust engine technologies resulting in the final prototype (XP984) being powered by the 15,000lb thrust Pegasus 5 engine. Interest from the USA and West Germany soon resulted in a tripartite agreement to conduct an operational evaluation of both the concept and the aircraft. Using XP984 as its model, Hawker Siddeley produced nine Kestrel FGA Mk 1s, which were tested at squadron operations level for six months in 1965, flying 1,367 sorties and suffering the loss of only one aeroplane. Just as the test programme launched, the British Ministry of Aviation (MoA) contracted for an improved version called the P.1127(RAF) based on the upgrade to Kestrel XS693 with the 19,000lb thrust Pegasus 6 engine. Now called the Harrier, the first of six developmental aircraft (XV276) flew on 31 March 1966. Early the following year the RAF ordered its first 60 Harrier GR 1s.

The first pre-production Hawker Siddeley Harrier, XV276, on a test flight at Dunsfold in 1966.

The cyclical, iterative development process allowed ship-board trials to be conducted during each of the three cycles. P.1127 prototype XP831 was landed aboard *Ark Royal* on 8 February 1963 while the vessel was anchored off Lyme Bay. The Kestrel had undertaken 'deck trials' aboard *Bulwark* in 1966 and two Harrier GR 1s completed compatibility evaluation aboard *Ark Royal*'s sister-ship, HMS *Eagle*, in March 1970, flying 58 sorties and resulting in No. 1(F) Sqn being cleared to operate from Royal Navy flightdecks, should the need arise. Consequently, in 1971, it was a natural outcome for the naval air staff to issue a requirement for a 'seagoing aircraft based on the RAF's [improved] Harrier GR 3', and Hawker Siddeley was contracted to develop a jet to fulfil that requirement. The type would have the primary roles of air defence, reconnaissance and maritime strike, the last using the new British Aircraft Corporation (later BAe Dynamics) Sea Eagle anti-ship missile as its primary weapon.

The 'ski-jump' takeoff ramp at RNAS Yeovilton became operational in February 1981, facilitating testing and training for shipboard operations. In April 1982, SHAR developmental aircraft XZ440 used the 'ski-jump' during trials for the dual AIM-9G/H underwing missile launch rails. (Paul Crickmore)

Sea Harrier FRS 1 ZA193 made its first flight on 13 January 1982 and was delivered to the Royal Navy 20 days later – it was originally held in storage at RAF St Athan, in Wales. On 3 April 1982, the day after Argentina repossessed the disputed islands, ZA193 was flown to RNAS Yeovilton to reinforce 800 NAS, which was embarked in HMS *Hermes* for the ensuing campaign. The aircraft's first combat mission was flown on 1 May, when Lt Cdr Mike Blissett was at the controls (callsign 'Black 3') as part of the strike on BAM Malvinas at Port Stanley/ Puerto Argentino airfield. The jet dropped three CBU canisters. On 24 May Lt Dave Smith used '93' to shoot down Capt Raúl Díaz's Dagger (C-430) with an AIM-9L north of Pebble Island/Isla Borbón. This aircraft returned to Britain aboard HMS *Hermes* in July 1982, and it was lost when the forward pitch nozzle control failed during landing approach to *Invincible* on 28 May 1992. RAF exchange pilot Flt Lt P. N. Wilson, serving with 800 NAS at the time, ejected from the aeroplane and was subsequently rescued.

The resulting Sea Harrier design included numerous basic changes to adapt the airframe to shipboard operations, such as replacement of magnesium and other components prone to salt-water corrosion with ones of corrosion-proof aluminium. To become a fighter, the cockpit was raised 11 inches and fitted with a bubble canopy, immensely improving all-round visibility, and a radar was added.

The primary air-to-air targets were Soviet naval aviation (*Aviatsiya Voenno-Morskogo Flota*, Aviation of the Military-Maritime Fleet or AV-MF) Tupolev Tu-95RT 'Bear-D' turboprop-powered maritime reconnaissance aircraft. In the event of the Cold War turning hot, AV-MF 'Bears' were expected to roam the North Atlantic and North and Norwegian Seas searching for NATO task forces. Once located, these 'snoopers' would shadow the targets and report position updates for waves of supersonic Tu-22K 'Blinder-Bs' and Tu-22M 'Backfire-Bs' with their large Raduga Kh-22 (AS-4 'Kitchen') and KSR-5 (AS-6 'Kingfish') Mach 3.5 nuclear-tipped anti-shipping cruise missiles. Since the decidedly subsonic Sea Harrier had no hope of catching the bombers or their missiles, their job was to intercept and destroy – or at least chase away – the shadowers, thus blinding the AV-MF attackers.

Since the 'Bear's' high altitude flight profile, its large size and its four giant contra-rotating propellers presented an excellent radar return at long ranges, only a small, low-power radar was needed. The 90kW Ferranti ARI.5979 'Sea Spray' surface search radar, which was already fielded by the Royal Navy's Westland Lynx HAS 2 naval attack helicopter to locate and illuminate surface targets – as small as patrol boats and fast attack craft – for the Sea Skua anti-ship missile, was considered adequate as an AI radar as well. Other modifications included the substitution of the GR 3's inertial navigation system with a Ferranti twin-gyro Attitude Reference Platform and Navigation computer that used a Decca 72 Doppler radar for constant updates, installation of a 0.75-second quicker Martin-Baker Mk 10H ejector seat, a new Smith Industries Heads Up Display (HUD) and a radio altimeter.

The design proposal put forward by Hawker Siddeley (nationalised as British Aerospace in 1977) was accepted and a contract for 24 Sea Harrier FRS 1s was signed in May 1975. The first three (XZ438, XZ439 and XZ440) were developmental airframes powered by the improved 21,500lb thrust Pegasus 11 Mk 104. By the time the first production aircraft flew on 20 August 1978, the contract had been increased to 34 aircraft, with deliveries to Royal Naval Air Station (RNAS) Yeovilton commencing with the arrival of XZ451 on 18 June 1979.

Meanwhile, in parallel with the SHAR's development, its carriers were also prepared. HMS *Invincible* was ordered in April 1973, the keel being laid three months later. Britain's newest carrier, now displacing 22,000 tons under full load, was launched on 3 May 1977. *Hermes* underwent further modification in 1976–77 during which a 12-degree 'ski jump' was mounted to the forward end of the flightdeck, allowing the launching of fully loaded SHARs, the ship now displacing 28,700 tons under full load. With *Invincible* commissioned in July 1980, *Bulwark* was placed in reserve status and decommissioned the following March. Meanwhile, in 1975, the Admiralty formally redesignated the (then) three 'through-deck cruisers' (a new *Ark Royal* was ordered in December 1978) as 'Command Cruisers', each to embark a squadron of six Sea Harriers, in addition to their complement of ASW helicopters.

SEA HARRIER FRS 1

46ft 3in

12ft 2in

27ft 3in

TECHNICAL SPECIFICATIONS

MIRAGE IIIEA

By the end of the 1960s – especially in the face of rapidly advancing aviation technologies of the day – the FAA realised that its air defence forces, based upon Korean War-vintage North American Aviation F-86F Sabres, were rapidly becoming obsolete. Deciding to replace its Sabres with the new high-performance Mirage III, Argentina ordered ten single-seat IIIEA interceptors and two IIIBA two-seat trainers. Eschewing the new variant's ground-attack capability, the FAA ordered its aircraft without the Marconi Doppler navigation radar and associated systems.

Deliveries began at Bordeaux in September 1972, with the new aircraft being ferried by FAA Lockheed C-130E Hercules (*Grupo 1 de Transporte Aéreo*) to Base Aérea Militar (BAM) Dr Mariano Moreno, 15nm (nautical miles) south of Buenos Aires. The first example (serial I-003) was assembled and test flown in January 1973. Flying activities began in July after the cadre of instructor pilots (IPs) returned from training in France, and the *I Escuadrón de Caza Interceptora* (1st Fighter Interceptor Squadron) was established that same month. The unit's mission was the air defence of the Argentine capital and, in December 1975, *VIII Brigada Aérea* (8th Air Brigade) was established at BAM Moreno, with *Grupo 8 de Caza* being the brigade's sole operational flying unit.

During the first decade of operations two Mirages – one single-seater and one dual – were lost when they departed controlled flight during high angle of attack (AOA) manoeuvring, resulting in unrecoverable flat spins. In both cases the pilots were able to eject safely, the events dramatically demonstrating the perils of dogfighting at high AOA in delta-wing jets. To replace these losses and to expand the group to two squadrons, seven more advanced Mirage IIIEAs were acquired in 1980.

The Mirage IIIEA was a truly modern, high-performance, all-weather interceptor. Powered by the 13,668lb thrust SNECMA Atar 09C-3 afterburning turbojet, it could attain Mach 2.2

at high altitudes. However, the Atar provided a relatively low thrust-to-weight ratio of 0.68 to 1, so it could only sustain 3–4g, depending on altitude. Consequently, the Mirage was a relatively poorly manoeuvring fighter if the pilot flew it to maintain its energy. However, if need be, its delta wing could generate one sharp turn (90° at low altitude/45–60° at higher levels) if maximum g was pulled while at high speed, enabling it to briefly point its weapons at a target or to overshoot an attacker, before the resulting rapid airspeed 'bleed-off' drained away its manoeuvring capability.

For the upcoming conflict, the Mirage IIIEA had one critical limitation. Even at high altitude the Atar was a prodigious 'gas guzzler', limiting the aircraft's effective combat radius to a maximum of 450nm. Although the Mirage could be equipped with a pair of non-jettisonable RPK100 500-litre (110 Imp/132 US gal) supersonic tanks, it could not reach the Malvinas with these, necessitating the use of large RP30 1,700-litre (375 gal) drop tanks. Using these, and flying from BAM Río Gallegos (428nm to the Malvinas), Mirage pilots would have a maximum of 12 minutes (at high altitude – only five minutes at low level) in the combat arena, according to the manufacturer's engineering data.

The Mirage's Thomson-CSF Cyrano II radar was designed to locate high-flying bombers beyond visual range. With a transmitting power of 200kW, this I/J-band monopulse system could detect a bomber-size target at a range of 21.5nm flying at or above the Mirage's altitude. Being a pulse AI radar, the Cyrano II lacked a 'look-down' capability, the target being hidden within its electronic 'ground clutter' returns. For engaging 'level to look-up' targets the radar's capabilities included search, lock-on (tracking) of designated targets and target illumination for Matra R 530E employment. Because its Cassegrain antenna was not gyro (i.e., horizontally) stabilised, effective search and any acquisitions (lock-ons) had to be made during wings-level flight, making the radar unusable in a dynamic, manoeuvring (dogfighting) environment.

The Cyrano II supported the Matra R 530E AAM, 51 of which were acquired by the FAA in both semi-active radar (SAR) homing and IR versions. Although significantly upgraded from its original 1962 form, the missile's effectiveness was limited to engaging large aircraft flying 'straight and level'. While its two-stage Hotchkiss-Brandt/SNPE Antoinette rocket motor could boost the missile to Mach 2.7 and sustain it for a range approximating ten nautical miles, depending on the intercept geometry, the R 530E

The FAA was proud to be the only Latin American air arm to acquire a supersonic interceptor. From the first batch of ten Mirage IIIEAs (plus two two-seat Mirage IIIBAs), I-012 is presented with the only missile the type was initially capable of carrying, the Matra R 530. As the Mirage IIIEA's primary weapon, the R 530, which had a 360-degree engagement envelope above 30,000ft, was limited to 'stern only' at lower altitudes. Designed to bring down a nuclear weapons-carrying bomber, it had limited effectiveness against small, highly manoeuvrable fighter-type targets. (Jorge Fazio)

was a heavy – 192kg (425lb) – projectile with extremely poor manoeuvrability, making it easily defeated by an agile adversary.

In addition to the R 530E, the FAA's second batch of Mirage IIIEAs could also employ the Matra R 550 Magic IR missile, the first shipment of which was received on 15 April 1982. The Magic was a highly manoeuvrable AAM, the AD3601 seeker head of which had a relatively wide field of view and high gimbal limits, near 90°. Larger than the comparable AIM-9, it had a greater range – approximately six nautical miles at medium/high

One of the seven more capable Mirage IIIEAs comprising the FAA's second batch, *Grupo 8 de Caza's* I-014 stands ready for a CAP mission over Islas Malvinas. It is seen armed with a recently received Matra R 550 Magic missile beneath the wingtip, as well as an R 530 in the shadows, mounted on the centreline. (Jorge Fazio)

altitudes – but was 'rear quarter' only (within 45° of the target's tail/hot jet exhaust), necessitating manoeuvring to a position behind the target in order to employ it. *Grupo 8 de Caza* pilots only started to train on this new weapon after the war had begun.

Overall, the Mirage IIIEA was at a serious disadvantage in the air superiority role over the Malvinas. To reach the islands and have enough fuel to return, it had to be flown in at high altitude – alerting anyone with a radar of its approach – and could not 'see' targets below that altitude. Therefore, its pilots were totally dependent upon ground control intercept (GCI) support from the FAA's Westinghouse AN/TPS-43F S-band long-range air control and warning radar that was based near Stanley Airfield (called BAM Malvinas by the Argentines). With an effective range of 200nm, altitude coverage up to 75,000ft and a ten-second data refresh rate, this powerful, robust system included IFF, ground clutter rejection and a digital moving target indicator that allowed the tracking of enemy aircraft – and control of friendly ones – throughout the area.

It was supplemented by an Argentine army ISC Cardion AN/TPS-44A long-range (100nm) surveillance radar tied to its Skyguard-directed 35mm Oerlikon AAA batteries. The inputs from these two systems were correlated in the *Centro de Información y Control* (Combat Information Centre or CIC) known as 'Radar Malvinas'.

DAGGER

To augment the sophisticated all-weather Mirage IIIEAs, Argentina purchased its first 26 Daggers (including two two-seaters) along with 50 Shafrir-2 missiles in December 1978, followed by 13 more (including two two-seaters) two years later. The FAA valued the type's substantial air-to-ground capabilities and purchased them to reinforce its ageing A-4B/C Skyhawks in the attack role, as well as to augment the Mirage IIIEA in the air defence role. Purchased as dual-role fighter-bombers, they equipped three squadrons of *VI Brigada Aérea/Grupo 6 de Caza* based at BAM Tandil, approximately 167nm south of Buenos Aires.

MIRAGE IIIEA MISSILES

The main armament of the Mirage IIIEA system originally consisted of two 30mm DEFA guns in an internal bay and a single R 530 radar-guided medium range missile. In 1981 the FAA's second batch of seven Mirage IIIEAs was received, and with them the short-range infrared Matra R 550 Magic I. Kits and wiring to upgrade the first batch of 12 aircraft were received afterwards, increasing the capabilities of the Argentine Mirages. The Matra R 530 was a semi-active radar-homing missile that was originally planned to be the sole missile armament of the Mirage. It was powered by a two-stage solid-propellant motor and

had to be guided by the pilot by keeping the target locked with the on-board Cyrano II radar. It was intended to shoot down slow and cumbersome bombers, being practically useless against fighters. Movement was controlled by fins in the tail area. The Matra R 550 Magic I was an infrared-guided missile for close-in combat that could manoeuvre up to 6g and reach speeds of more than 700 knots. With movements controlled by canard wings, the missile could engage the target independently from the firing aircraft. Magic I was the main armament of the Argentine Mirage IIIEA fleet during the war.

Aft of the cockpit, the airframe was structurally identical to the Mirage IIIE, but the 20.75-in longer nose and the absence of the bulky, heavy Cyrano II radar allowed other avionics to be repositioned forward, providing increased fuel tankage aft of the cockpit. The latter boosted its effective combat radius to 500nm and increased its 'on station time' by about five minutes over that of the Mirage IIIEA. The performance of the Mirage and Dagger were virtually identical, with the latter being only 221lb lighter. Having the same wings, but lower combat weight, the Dagger had a slightly better wing loading and a thrust-to-weight ratio of 0.706 to 1, so it accelerated faster, could sustain its energy longer in a turning fight and was slightly more manoeuvrable than its progenitor, especially at low altitudes.

While the Dagger had a nominally better 'time over target' than the Mirage, its air-to-air warload was limited to a pair of Rafael Shafrir-2 ('Dragonfly') IR missiles and two 30mm cannon. The Shafrir-2 was an Israeli copy of the early Raytheon AIM-9D Sidewinder with a more restricted, stern-only (within 30° of the target's tail) employment envelope. Its effective range was 10,500ft at high altitude, reducing to 6,000ft at medium altitude and shrinking to about 3,500ft at low altitude – its minimum range was 330ft.

Originally intended as a back-up to the Matra missiles, both the Mirage III and 5J/Nesher/Dagger also mounted a pair of Direction des Études et Fabrications d'Armement (DEFA) 30mm revolver cannon, each with 125 rounds, carried in a ventral tray, with the muzzles located on the undersides of the engine air intakes. The

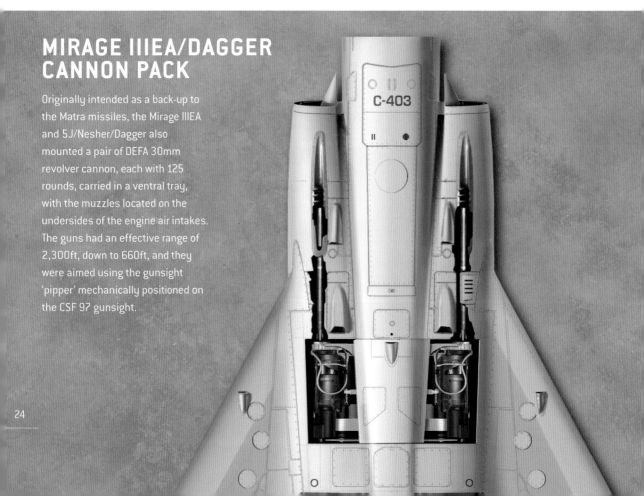

MIRAGE IIIEA/DAGGER CANNON PACK

Originally intended as a back-up to the Matra missiles, the Mirage IIIEA and 5J/Nesher/Dagger also mounted a pair of DEFA 30mm revolver cannon, each with 125 rounds, carried in a ventral tray, with the muzzles located on the undersides of the engine air intakes. The guns had an effective range of 2,300ft, down to 660ft, and they were aimed using the gunsight 'pipper' mechanically positioned on the CSF 97 gunsight.

guns had an effective range of 2,300ft, down to 660ft, and they were aimed using the gunsight 'pipper' mechanically positioned on the CSF 97 gunsight. Dagger pilots had to use visual range estimation, and they set the gyro-stabilised gunsight using stadiametric ranging by twisting the throttle grip when it came to aiming the cannons.

The Dagger had an impressive load-carrying capability, reduced somewhat by the need to carry two 1,300- or 1,700-litre drop tanks on the main wing

A line up of recently arrived Daggers at BAM Tandil in December 1982. Only a few have had the *Grupo VI* badge applied to the tail and the IFF antenna on the tail is still not installed, although the support base is visible. (Guillermo Posadas)

stations. When the two under wingtip stations were used for AAMs, there remained the centreline station, which could carry one or two bombs, and two rear under-fuselage stations mounted beneath the aft wing root. Together these could carry up to four 250kg (550lb) or 400kg (880lb) general-purpose bombs or Belouga cluster bombs, while up to four JL100 combined fuel/rocket pods, or Matra Type 155 rocket pods (18 x 68mm SNEB rockets each) could be carried on the underwing stations.

Typically for the FAA's maritime strike missions the Daggers would be loaded with two 250kg (550lb) bombs on the rear under-fuselage stations or a single 500kg (1,100lb) bomb mounted on the centreline. Most effective for low-level deliveries were the Spanish-built Explosivos Alaveses, S.A. (EXPAL) BRP-250 250kg (550lb) parachute-retarded bombs, although, in the event, numerous times BR-250 or British Mk 17 1,000lb 'slick' (unretarded) bombs would be carried instead.

For anti-ship strike missions, Daggers were typically armed with two bombs on the aft fuselage stations or two on the centreline. Loaded with four 550lb BR-250s, C432 is prepared for its 4 June 1982 mission against British forces approaching Mount Kent. (Guillermo Posadas)

SEA HARRIER FRS 1

To protect fleet elements from Soviet long-range maritime strike aircraft and their air-launched cruise missiles, the Royal Navy had developed a 'layered defence' consisting of three rings. The outer ring was composed of Combat Air Patrols (CAPs) manned by two-ship formations of fighters positioned 60nm 'up-threat' – towards the anticipated threat source/direction – alerted and vectored to the approaching targets by controllers aboard 'radar picket ships'.

Typically, the 'radar picket ships' were Type 42 destroyers stationed about halfway between the CAPs and the task force, giving the fighters plenty of space to intercept and engage the targets before entering the surface-to-air missile (SAM) envelopes

HMS *Invincible* launches a SHAR. For the last two decades of the 20th Century the Royal Navy's fleet air defence would be built around 'Command Cruisers', each embarking a squadron of Sea Harriers and armed with a GWS 30 Sea Dart medium range SAM system.

of these destroyers or the close escorts, usually frigates, of the task force itself. The middle layer of air defence was formed by Hawker Siddeley's Guided Weapons System (GWS) 30 Sea Dart medium-range SAMs aboard the picket destroyers. The inner ring consisted of Short Brothers & Harland GWS 20/22/24 Seacat and British Aerospace GWS 25 Sea Wolf short-range SAMs mounted on destroyers, frigates and the carriers themselves, along with each ship's turreted 4.5in (114mm) multipurpose and manually aimed 20mm and/or 40mm AAA weapons.

SHAR CAPs were normally controlled from a destroyer's – usually the designated Anti-Air Warfare Control (AAWC) ship – operations room (Ops Room) using the ship's Type 965 surveillance radar. This system could see high-altitude (above 20,000ft) targets out to 150nm, but its effective range shrank as altitude decreased, with its low-level look limited to 15nm. Additionally, anticipating combat only over the open ocean, the Type 965 lacked modern, effective, ground clutter filters that permitted the tracking of aircraft over land.

Once on CAP, SHAR pilots would loiter until given an initial vector – bearing and range, and altitude if known – to search for the 'snooper' or intercept an incoming attack. To find its adversaries, the SHAR mounted the small Ferranti Blue Fox radar – an I-band monopulse system that could locate a bomber-size target at 40nm range and could detect a fighter-size target at 18nm in the 'level to look up' mode. Not anticipating over-land operations, the Blue Fox had none of the advancing pulse-Doppler technology of the day and, consequently, had no 'look down' search/track capability. This meant that it was awash with 'ground clutter' at low altitude over land or rough seas. As one SHAR pilot put it, it:

suffered terribly from ground returns, or clutter, over land, but worked fairly well at medium to high levels over the sea. At low level it was useless over land, and it required a lot of skilful handling over water to pick up and track a target . . . In such conditions it was possible to pick up low-level targets at a range of 15 miles or so, but it required a great deal of heads-in [cockpit] work on the radar scope.

Even though it was originally intended that the SHAR's primary targets were large, subsonic Soviet bombers, the FRS 1 proved surprisingly agile and very adept at air-to-air manoeuvring against opposing fighters. Its exceptional thrust-to-weight ratio – 1.23:1 – allowed it to sustain much higher gs, with correspondingly tighter turning circles, than its opponents, at least at low altitude. However, performance of the Pegasus Mk 104 turbofan fell off markedly as altitude increased, limiting the SHAR's advantage to below 15,000ft. Consequently, if the SHAR pilot could lure the Mirage/Dagger down to his altitude, negating the enemy's performance advantage and enhancing his own, the Sea Harrier proved more than a match in a manoeuvring fight.

Normally, the SHAR's primary weapon was the Raytheon AIM-9G/H Sidewinder missile, which was an improved version of the US Navy's AIM-9D used with limited success (17.9 per cent effectiveness) in the Vietnam War. The AIM-9G had a new forward canard design that improved manoeuvring performance, thus expanding the engagement envelope to approximately 45 degrees off the tail. Assuming co-equal speeds of fighter and target, the missile's maximum range at medium altitudes was about 9,000ft or 1.5nm.

With the onset of hostilities with Argentina, the Royal Navy requisitioned 200 vastly improved AIM-9Ls from the US Navy. The '9-Lima' was breakthrough technology because of its new optical system (an Argon-cooled Indium Antimonide detector element with much more discriminating IR sensitivity) and DSU-15A/B active laser fuse that detonated the warhead before target passage. This allowed SHAR pilots to employ the AIM-9L from any aspect – including 'head on' – rather than having to manoeuvre to the 'six o'clock' to use their missile.

Additionally, the SHAR mounted two Armament Development Establishment/ Enfield (ADEN) Mk 5 30mm revolver cannon in ventral pods, with 120 rounds per gun, for both air-to-air gunnery and air-to-ground strafing. For its reconnaissance

800 NAS SHAR '123' (XZ492) in flight, carrying its full combat fit – two 100 gal (455-litre) drop tanks, two AIM-9G Sidewinders and a pair of ADEN 30mm cannon pods. This aeroplane was subsequently credited with an A-4C victory on 21 May 1982, its pilot, Lt Cdr Neil Thomas of 899 NAS (who had been seconded to 800 NAS), destroying the Skyhawk with an AIM-9L.

Raytheon AIM-9L mounted on a Sea Harrier FRS 1 LAU-7A/5 underwing launcher rail. (Tim Callaway Collection)

SEA HARRIER FRS 1 ARMAMENT

The main armament of the Sea Harrier FRS 1 was two Raytheon AIM-9L Sidewinder heat-seeking missiles carried on underwing pylons, augmented by two ADEN 30mm gun pods mounted beneath the fuselage. The 'Limas' had been supplied by the USA to the British Task Force during its journey to the South Atlantic. The latest version of the Sidewinder missile, the AIM-9L was the first 'all-aspect' IR weapon with the ability to be fired from all directions, including head-on, which had a dramatic effect on close-in combat tactics. The much improved performance of this missile gave the SHAR pilots an insuperable advantage over their Argentine counterparts, whose armament forced them to fire their weapons from almost directly behind their foes, whereas the envelope of the new Sidewinder permitted a more ample angle of firing. The SHAR was also fitted with two Armament Development Establishment/ Enfield (ADEN) Mk 5 30mm revolver cannon in ventral pods, with 120 rounds per gun, mounted beneath its fuselage. These weapons were used for both air-to-air gunnery and air-to-ground strafing during the fighting in 1982. Indeed, three Argentine aircraft were brought down by 30mm cannon rounds fired by SHARs.

mission, the aircraft was fitted with an oblique F.95 camera on the starboard side, and for the strike role it was equipped to deliver the WE177 nuclear bomb. For conventional air-to-ground attacks, the jet could employ two-inch RP rocket pods or drop 1,000lb high explosive/medium capacity (HEMC) bombs and Hunting Engineering Ltd BL755 cluster munitions using level ('lay-down'), dive-bombing and 'loft' or 'toss' deliveries. A small 20K-word digital weapons aiming computer converted the radar's range, angles and closure data and presented weapons delivery/employment symbology to the pilot via the HUD.

Finally, although the SHAR was not equipped with active or passive electronic countermeasures (ECM), it did have a 360-degree Marconi ARI.18223 radar warning receiver (RWR). As an expedient, the only ECM available to the SHAR pilot was to stow 'bundles of chaff' – thin strips of metal foil that would blossom in the airstream and attract tracking radars away from an aircraft – in the ventral speedbrake well and deploy them (by opening the speedbrake) when the ARI.16223 indicated a radar missile lock-on.

Sea Harrier FRS 1, Mirage IIIEA and Dagger Comparison Specifications

	Sea Harrier FRS 1	Mirage IIIEA	Dagger A
Powerplant	21,500lb thrust Rolls-Royce Pegasus Mk 104	13,668lb thrust SNECMA Atar 09C-3	13,668lb thrust SNECMA Atar 09C-3
Dimensions			
Wingspan	27ft 3in	26ft 11.5in	26ft 11.5in
Length	46ft 3in	49ft 3.5in	51ft 0.5in
Height	12ft 2in	13ft 11.5in	13ft 11.5in
Wing Area	201.1 sq. ft	375.13 sq. ft	375.13 sq. ft
Weight			
Empty	14,500lb	15,542lb	15,763lb
Loaded	26,500lb	30,203lb	30,203lb
Thrust-to-Weight*	1.23:1	0.68:1	0.71:1
Wing Loading*	87.0lb/sq. ft	53.3lb/sq. ft	51.6lb/sq. ft
Performance			
Maximum Speed	626 knots at sea level	750 knots at sea level	744 knots at sea level
Maximum Mach	1.25	2.2	2.2
Combat Radius	300nm	450nm	500nm
Initial Climb Rate	8,200ft/min	12,030ft/min	12,303ft/min
Service Ceiling	51,200ft	55,744ft	47,200ft
Armament	2 x 30mm ADEN cannon 2 x AIM-9L IR missiles	2 x 30mm DEFA 552 cannon 1 x MATRA R 530E and/or 2 x MATRA R 550	2 x 30mm DEFA 552 cannon 2 x Rafael Shafrir-2 IR missiles
Radar/Fire Control System (ranges for bomber-size target)	Ferranti Blue Fox (40nm range)	Thomson-CSF Cyrano II (25nm range)	None

Note – Thrust-to-Weight Ratio and Wing Loading calculations use 'combat weight', which is after external tanks and air-to-ground ordnance are jettisoned, 60 per cent internal fuel remaining, with full air-to-air ordnance load (air-to-air missiles and gun ammunition). Thrust is calculated at sea level.

THE STRATEGIC SITUATION

It is well beyond the scope of this small study to discuss the sovereignty dispute that underpinned the South Atlantic conflict of 1982. Suffice it to say that – because both sides claimed the islands – the issue devolved to the matter of possession. Britain had possessed the islands since 1833, but the MoD's 1981 Defence White Paper gave Argentina's ruling *Junta* some hope that, in the ongoing negotiations, they would be returned to Argentina before the 150-year anniversary of the event. Published in June 1981, 'The UK Defence Programme: The Way Forward' was a major review of Britain's defence policy designed to reduce expenditure to better afford supporting NATO at the expense of 'out of area operations'. Part of this cost reduction programme was to be the retirement of the Falklands-based icebreaker/patrol vessel HMS *Endurance* (as of 15 April 1982) and withdrawing the 43-man Royal Marines detachment (Naval Party 8901) from the islands.

To the *Junta* leadership, the White Paper was considered a clear 'signal' that the British government wished to rid itself of one of the last vestiges of its colonial empire. With the sovereignty dispute negotiations deadlocked, it appeared to President and army commander-in-chief Teniente General (Lieutenant General) Leopoldo Fortunato Galtieri and the commander of the Argentine Navy, Almirante (Admiral) Jorge Isaac Anaya, that they were being presented with an opportunity to repossess the islands.

In March 1982, a 41-man salvage team recovering 60 million pounds of scrap metal from three abandoned whaling stations on South Georgia Island (a Falklands Islands Dependency) raised the Argentine flag over its camp. An affront to British authority, the situation escalated rapidly, with both sides sending naval auxiliaries and marines to South Georgia in what initially appeared to be a 'stand-off' confrontation.

Consequently, the *Junta* decided to proceed with Operación *Rosario*, an amphibious landing that repossessed Islas Malvinas on 2 April and Isla San Pedro (South Georgia Island) the following day. Confident that the British government would find a military operation to recover the islands too intimidating and expensive to undertake, the *Junta* members were both surprised and ill prepared for the British reaction. Unwilling to accept the *fait accompli*, British Prime Minister Margaret Thatcher ordered an immediate military response, authorising the formation of a carrier and amphibious 'task force to repossess the Falkland Islands as quickly as possible'.

Comprised of aircraft carriers HMS *Hermes* (flagship) and HMS *Invincible*, the carrier task group steamed from Portsmouth on 5 April. They embarked, respectively, 800 NAS and 801 NAS, totalling 20 Sea Harriers. This force joined Rear Admiral John Forester 'Sandy' Woodward's First Destroyer Flotilla – five destroyers and three frigates – at Ascension Island and was quickly reorganised into carrier Task Group (TG) 317.8 and placed under Woodward's command. A surface action sub-unit (TG 317.8.2) of three Type 42 destroyers and two frigates was sent to the South Atlantic to enforce the 200nm Maritime Exclusion Zone instituted on 12 April.

The main body – two carriers, four destroyers and frigates and three Royal Fleet Auxiliaries (RFAs) – departed Ascension on 18 April to join the surface action unit, while another task group (TG 317.9) headed further south to recover South Georgia Island. The latter group – one destroyer, one frigate, an RFA and *Endurance* – arrived offshore, and in a sharp action a week later repossessed the island, capturing 135 Argentine soldiers and sailors and disabling and capturing the submarine *Santa Fe*.

Despite the fact that the FAA lacked a maritime reconnaissance capability, beginning on 21 April it employed its two Boeing 707-320Cs (*Grupo 1 de Transporte Aéreo*) to locate Woodward's carrier task group using the aircraft's weather radar with visual confirmation. First located some 700nm south of Ascension, these *ad hoc* maritime reconnaissance missions monitored TG 317.8's southward progress for the next four days. Each day the 800 NAS 'alert jet' intercepted the 'shadower' – just as the SHAR was designed to do – but no shots were fired. After a diplomatic warning that the military airliner would 'be regarded as hostile and . . . dealt with accordingly', and with the firefight on South Georgia signalling British intent to use lethal force, the FAA decided to be 'less assertive' in maritime reconnaissance operations after 25 April. During the nights of 27 and 30 April, using its radar the Boeing 707 crew determined that the British fleet was 'loitering' well east of the islands.

To meet the surprising British response, on 7 April the *Junta* established the joint-service *Teatro de Operaciones del Atlántico Sur* (South Atlantic Theatre of Operations or TOAS), headquartered at BAM Comodoro Rivadavia, with the chief of naval operations, Vicealmirante (Vice Admiral) Juan Lombardo, as commander. The FAA's component was *Comando Fuerza Aérea Sur* (CdoFAS or Southern Air Command) under Brigadier Ernesto Horacio Crespo, commander of *IV Brigada Aérea*.

To Crespo's command were assigned portions of the FAA's five high-performance fighter, fighter-bomber and bomber units. For air defence of TOAS headquarters and air superiority over the islands, *Grupo 8 de Caza* deployed five older Mirage IIIEAs to BAM Rivadavia and six more-capable (Magic-carrying) 'second batch' interceptors to BAM Río Gallegos. Leaving *Escuadrón I* at Tandil to continue training and logistics support, *Grupo 6 de Caza's Escuadrón II Aeromóvil* (nicknamed

Flown by Vicecomodoro (Wing Commander/Lieutenant Colonel equivalent) Luis Litrenta, KC-130H Hercules TC-70 of *Grupo 1 de Transporte Aéreo* leads the first flight of four Pucaras from *Grupo 7 de Ataque* to land on Islas Malvinas on 2 April 1982 as part of Operación *Rosario*. (Luis Litrenta)

'La Marinete') deployed nine Daggers to the rather austere BAM San Julián and *Escuadrón III Aeromóvil* ('Avutardas Salvajes') sent nine more to Base Aeronaval (BAN) Río Grande, on the southern tip of Argentina. These were augmented by 11 *Grupo 4 de Caza* A-4Cs flying from BAM San Julián and 22 *Grupo 5 de Caza* A-4Bs based at BAM Río Gallegos. *Grupo 2 Bombardeo* had eight serviceable twin-engined Canberra B 62 jet bombers that would operate from BAN Almirante Marcos Zar, at Trelew.

The island was defended by the joint *Guarnición Militar Malvinas* (Malvinas Military Garrison) commanded by General de Brigada (Brigadier General) Mario Benjamín Menéndez. The garrison consisted of Menéndez's 9,800-man *Agrupación de Ejército Malvinas* (Malvinas Army Group) composed of two reinforced mechanised brigades, supported by 19 helicopters. The air component was the *Agrupación Fuerza Aérea Malvinas* (Malvinas Air Force Group) under Brigadier Luis Castellano. It

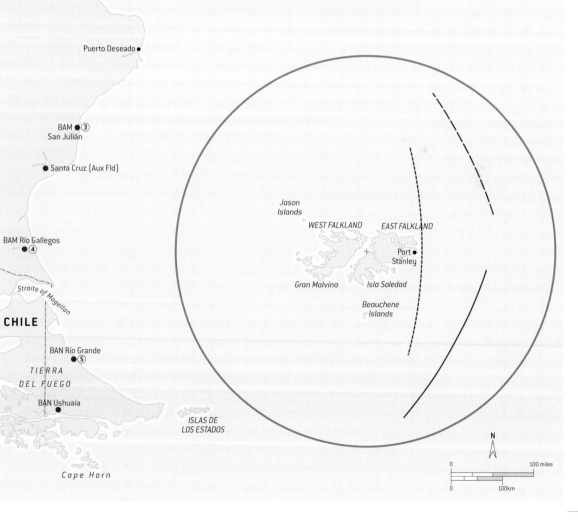

Legend

- ● Air Bases
- ── 200NM Total Exclusion Zone
- ── Dagger Combat Radius from BAM San Julián
- – – Dagger Combat Radius from BAN Río Grande
- ---- Mirage IIIEA Combat Radius from BAM Río Gallegos

Argentine Air Combat Units:
1. BAN Almirante Marcos Zar, Trelew
   Grupo 2 de Bombardeo – 8 Canberra B 62/T 64s
2. BAM Comodoro Rivadavia, HQ TAOS
   Grupo 8 de Caza – 5 Mirage IIIEAs (Air Defence only)
3. BAM San Julián
   Grupo 4 de Caza – 11 A-4C Skyhawks
   Grupo 6 de Caza – 9 Daggers
4. BAM Río Gallegos
   Grupo 5 de Caza – 22 A-4B Skyhawks
   Grupo 8 de Caza – 6 Mirage IIIEAs
5. BAN Contraalmirante Hermes Quijada, Río Grande
   Grupo 6 de Caza – 9 Daggers
   COAN *1era Escuadrilla de Ataque* – 6 MB.326GB/MB.339As
   COAN *2da Escuadrilla de Caza y Ataque* – 4 Super Étendards
   COAN *3era Escuadrilla de Caza y Ataque* – 8 A-4Q Skyhawks

RN Task Group 317.8 Sea Harrier FRS 1 Carriers, Units and Strength
HMS *Hermes*:
   800 NAS – 12 Sea Harrier FRS 1s
HMS *Invincible*:
   801 NAS – 8 Sea Harrier FRS 1s

BAN Almirante Zar, Trelew ● ①

ARGENTINA

BAM Comodoro
Rivadavia ● ②

Puerto Deseado ●

BAM ● ③
San Julián

● Santa Cruz (Aux Fld)

BAM Río Gallegos
● ④

Straits of Magellan

CHILE

BAN Río Grande ● ⑤

*TIERRA
DEL FUEGO*

● BAN Ushuaia

*ISLAS DE
LOS ESTADOS*

Cape Horn

Jason
Islands

WEST FALKLAND   EAST FALKLAND

Port ●
Stanley

Gran Malvina   *Isla Soledad*

Beauchene
Islands

N

| 0 | | | 100 miles |
| 0 | | | 100km |

consisted of 12 FMA IA 58 Pucará twin-turboprop light attack aircraft (*Grupo 7 de Ataque*) and four helicopters, augmented by four COAN Beechcraft T-34C-1 Turbo-Mentor armed trainers and four (later six) Aermacchi MB 339A light strike jets.

While these various joint organisations sound quite progressive, this was 'a first' in Argentine military history. Historically, the three services were constant rivals, and each jealously guarded its own areas of responsibilities. In 1969, the military dictatorship of General Juan Carlos Onganía directed that the navy had 'exclusive jurisdiction to defend Argentina from sea attack' and 'specifically prohibited the air force from developing or acquiring any capability suitable for aerial operations over the sea'. Consequently, not only did the FAA lack a real maritime reconnaissance capability, its fighter-bomber and bomber units had never practised anti-ship attacks.

Now, of course, to deal with the approaching British task force, an FAA maritime strike capability was desperately needed. To facilitate this, the navy conducted exercises from 17 to 25 April, including practising defending against air attacks. This allowed the FAA fighter-bomber units to practise attacking ships, especially the navy's two Type 42 destroyers *Santísima Trinidad* and *Hércules*. When using normal approach and attack parameters, the Dagger and Skyhawk pilots were detected and 'shot down' every time, but when one Dagger overflew the destroyers at ultra-low height as a parting salutation it was discovered that the on-board systems had not 'seen' the aircraft. This new approach inhibited the ship's ability to acquire a radar lock and firing solution. Subsequent practice showed it was successful in permitting 75 per cent of the 'attackers' to deliver ordnance without being engaged by the Type 42's anti-aircraft systems.

With tactics determined and training completed, the FAA units deployed to their operational bases, described earlier in this chapter. During this period Woodward's carrier task group was joined by the surface action group, and he remained east of the islands waiting for the British government – upon failure of diplomacy to defuse the situation – to send orders for him to proceed with combat operations.

THE COMBATANTS

ROYAL NAVY SEA HARRIER PILOT TRAINING

The nearly 30 SHAR pilots manning 800 and 801 NASs were a 'mixed bag'. About half of them were veteran Fleet Air Arm pilots from the *Ark Royal's* Phantom II, Buccaneer and (yes, even) Sea King squadrons, while another third were 'nuggets' (new pilots) who had just completed operational training with 899 NAS at RNAS Yeovilton. The rest were experienced RAF Harrier GR 3 'exchange pilots' – as well as the odd ex-RAF pilot who had transferred to the navy to fly SHARs – augmenting the Royal Navy's two new operational fighter squadrons.

SHAR students flew in the right seat of 899 NAS's Hunter T 8Ms during their Blue Fox radar training. Note the AIM-9 'training round' beneath the left wing. (Arie van Groen)

SEA HARRIER FRS 1 COCKPIT

1. Radar hand controller
2. Throttle
3. Nozzle selector
4. Undercarriage selector/lights
5. Flap selector lever
6. Water injection switch
7. PTR 377 UHF/VHF radio panel
8. Weapons control panel
9. Radar control panel
10. HUD control panel
11. G meter
12. Angle-of-attack indicator
13. Tachometer
14. Air-to-air missile controls
15. Barometric altimeter
16. Radio compass
17. Radar altimeter
18. Artificial horizon indicator
19. Emergency warning lights
20. Precautionary warning lights
21. Heads Up Display (HUD)
22. Ferranti Blue Fox radar display
23. Radar display controls
24. Vertical speed indicator
25. Fuel flow meter
26. Fuel gauge
27. Camera switches
28. Marconi ARI.18223 Radar
    Warning Receiver
29. Fire extinguisher button
30. Electrics and fuel control panel
31. IFF transponder
32. Navigation computer controls
    and display
33. Communications control panel
34. TACAN control panel
35. I-band transponder
36. Martin-Baker Mk 10H ejector seat
37. Ejection seat hand grip
38. Rudder pedals
39. Control column
40. Air speed indicator
41. Jet pipe temperature
42. Adjustable cockpit vents
43. Hydraulic systems gauges

The newest Sea Harrier pilots typically began learning their new 'trade' by attending the RAF's Tactical Weapons Unit (TWU), flying BAe Hawk T 1s (of No. 79 Sqn), from RAF Brawdy in Wales. After becoming familiar with basic air-to-ground weapons deliveries, basic fighter manoeuvres (BFM) and low-level navigation, the SHAR trainees reported to RAF Wittering, in Cambridgeshire, for VTOL training with No. 233 Operational Conversion Unit (OCU).

To pay for 'its share', the Royal Navy funded one of No. 233 OCU's two-seat Harrier T 4A (XW927) trainers that early SHAR trainees flew during the first three months of the seven-month course that taught them the basics of flying the 'jump jet'. Flying with B (for 'Basic') Flight, the trainee began with 'normal takeoffs and landings', the Harrier's small wing and high wing loading making the latter a lot like landing the Lockheed F-104 Starfighter – flying finals at 170 knots. The most challenging aspect of flying the new and unique fighter was, of course, VTOL, and the transition to and from wing-borne flight from/to that sustained by the Pegasus engine and its vectored thrust. While most landings were made with 60-degree downward nozzle deflection (using the 'land, then stop' technique), coming aboard ship required vertical ('stop, then land') approaches. Once the VTOLs – and transitions to/from them – were mastered, trainees practiced formation, instrument flying and BFM. From the three-month 'B-course', the SHAR trainee typically graduated with 28 hours of Harrier flying time before moving to Yeovilton.

In July 1979 the Royal Navy's Harrier T 4 was detached to Yeovilton, where it was initially assigned to 700A Intensive Flying Trails Unit (IFTU), joining five Sea Harriers used to develop procedures for ship-board V/STOL operations, embarked in HMS *Hermes*. On 31 March the following year IFTU was designated 899 NAS as the SHAR's 'Headquarters and Training Unit', and it began receiving graduates from the TWU. Eventually, this unit possessed up to 12 FRS 1s, with its two-seater being augmented by three loaned RAF Harrier T 4s (XW933, XW934 and XZ147) before the Royal Navy's dedicated T 4Ns (ZB604, ZB605 and ZB606) began arriving in September 1983.

For Blue Fox radar instruction, 899 NAS was later assigned three Hawker Hunter T 8Ms (XL580, XL602 and XL603), two of which had previously been used as flying testbeds for developing the system – one flew with Hawker Siddeley and the other was used by the Royal Radar Establishment. The aircraft's dual, side-by-side cockpit was modified through the installation of radar controls that allowed the SHAR trainee to learn to operate Blue Fox while the instructor flew the aircraft, providing about eight hours of airborne 'radar training'. Typically, the newly minted SHAR pilot graduated from the conversion course having flown 11 hours of dual instruction in the T 4N and another 72 hours in the FRS 1.

FAA MIRAGE/DAGGER PILOT TRAINING

Only the most experienced FAA pilots were initially introduced to the new Mirage IIIEA. A cadre of six veteran pilots was sent to France in late 1971, where the pilots learned to fly the Mirage IIIBA with ECT 2/2 'Côte d' Or' at Dijon-Longvic

Lt Raúl Díaz (right) was one of six Argentine Dagger pilots who learned to fly the Mirage 5P in secret with the *Fuerza Aérea del Perú's Escuadrón de Caza Interceptor 611* at Base Aérea Quinones Gonzalez, Chiclayo. (Raúl Díaz)

AB and where they received 12–13 hours of dual instruction before soloing in the Mirage IIIEA. The six then moved to EC 1/13 'Artois' at Colmar-Meyenheim AB, where they were instructed in combat techniques and weapons employment, three of them remaining for further training to become Mirage IIIEA instructors.

Seven years later, when the first Dagger squadron was activated, it was formed using highly experienced pilots from the two A-4B/C units (*Grupos 4* and *5 de Caza*) and Mirage IIIEA pilots from *Grupo 8 de Caza*. Three groups of pilots were organised – six were trained in Argentina using the Mirage IIIDA/EA, six more flew the Mirage 5P/DP with the Peruvian Air Force's *Escuadrón de Caza Interceptor 611* and the third group was split into two sections for training in Israel on the newly acquired Daggers.

Initially, the FAA sent four highly experienced Mirage IIIEA pilots to Israel to become qualified on the Nesher/Dagger, which included training in advanced air combat tactics with the IDF/AF. They received classroom instruction in all theoretical aspects of flying the new fighter-bomber, followed by flight instruction – both dual and solo – in instrument flying, formation, air-to-air and air-to-ground fundamentals, night flying, navigation and weapons deliveries. The Israeli instructors were combat veterans, several of them having been awarded aerial victories. The jets flown were the recently purchased Daggers that still sported Israeli camouflage and insignia. Experienced Mirage pilots, the Argentines flew only 2–2.5 hours of dual before their first solo in the Dagger. Upon returning to Argentina they became Dagger flight instructors, and were replaced in Israel by the second batch of trainees who became 'line pilots'.

Pilots that flew in Israel appreciated the differences between Israeli training and that provided in France. As one said later:

> The French school was different from the Israeli. As an example, the first would never allow the pilots to fly below 180 knots, while the Israelis, more experienced in close combat against the Arabs, used extreme [edges of the] flight envelopes. Their tactics were more aggressive and unorthodox. The Israelis were used to manoeuvres beyond the maximum-allowed performance by the French, who considered these transgressions forbidden.

The Israeli training occurred under maximum secrecy, with the Argentine pilots travelling as civilians in commercial airliners. The training in Peru was also conducted under the same strict security measures. At Base Aérea Quinones Gonzalez, the six trainees began with theoretical instruction, followed by ten dual flights of about 30 minutes each. After soloing, they returned to Argentina in October 1978. By the end of that year all three groups of pilots destined to fly the Dagger had returned to Argentina, joining the *Escuadrón Dagger* that had been established in August 1978 as part of *VIII Brigada Aérea*.

DAGGER COCKPIT

1. Anti-g suit connection and valve
2. Fuel control panel
3. VHF control panel
4. Interior/exterior lightning controls
5. UHF 1 and 2 radio controls
6. Throttle control
7. VOR navigation radio controls
8. Landing gear handle and indicator lights
9. Emergency landing gear handle
10. Emergency stores jettison panel
11. Drag chute release handle
12. Vertical speed indicator
13. Instrument panel lights
14. Airspeed/Mach indicator
15. Altimeter
16. Landing gear position lights
17. Emergency artificial horizon
18. G meter

19. CSF 97 gunsight
20. Clock
21. Standby magnetic compass
22. Gun camera
23. Engine/afterburner lights
24. Interconnection valve switch
25. Attitude direction indicator
26. Radio compass heading indicator
27. Exhaust gas temperature gauge
28. Engine tachometer
29. Emergency malfunction warning lights
30. Precautionary malfunction lights
31. Canopy locking lever
32. Dual hydraulic pressure indicators
33. Bombing programmer
34. Weapons control panel
35. Gun/missile control panel
36. Gyroscope centring control panel
37. Cockpit air conditioner control panel

38. Radio compass control panel
39. Control column
40. Martin-Baker Mk 6 zero-zero pilot seat
41. Ejection seat hand grip
42. Rudder pedals
43. Interior light
44. Landing gear not extended light
45. IFF control box
46. Fuel quantity indicator
47. Circuit breaker panel
48. Pressurisation control handle
49. Emergency brake handle
50. Automatic flight control panel
51. Air brake warning light
52. Fuel re-totaliser
53. RadioGoniometer (radio-based Direction Finder)
54. Intake shock cone position indicator

SEA HARRIER TACTICS

Originally developed to 'Hack the Shad' ('shoot down the shadower'), the SHAR quickly proved to be a potent fighter – with certain visual-only weapons limitations – against opposing air-to-air fighters and for intercepting fighter-bombers attacking the task force. Individual training engagements had been practised against most NATO nations' fighter types and, during NATO exercises, many SHAR pilots gained experience intercepting fighter-bombers attempting to attack their carrier. Consequently, once the carrier task group headed south to challenge Argentinian possession of the islands, tactics had already been developed for countering the anticipated threat to the fleet.

The basic fighting unit was a pair of SHARs that 'CAPed' at an altitude of 12,000–15,000ft, line abreast, with 800 yards spread. This was called 'battle formation'. As many as three two-ship CAPs would be positioned on the 'threat side' of the task group, with the centre CAP on the anticipated threat axis and the others displaced 40–60° to the flanks. When the AAWC ship detected a raid inbound – anticipating four/six/eight-ship formations at medium (15,000–20,000ft) altitude – the radar controller would vector the nearest formation to attack the inbound attackers 'head on'.

Using the AIM-9L, 800 and 801 NASs planned to have the SHAR flight leader attack one of the strike package leaders in the front quarter and 'blow through', while his wingman offset to one side and 'hooked' back towards the targets to attack the trailing fighter-bombers from astern. The other SHAR two-ships would be vectored to cut-off and attack the strikers from the flanks.

Designated as the primary air-to-air unit, 801 NAS, led by Lt Cdr Nigel D. 'Sharkey' Ward, anticipated the maritime strike forces at medium altitudes to be following COAN *2da Escuadrilla de Aeronaval de Caza y Ataque* Dassault Super Etendards ('SUEs'). The latter, armed with Exocet anti-ship missiles, would know the approximate location of the task group from coordinating with radar-equipped *Escuadra Aeronaval 2*'s Lockheed SP-2H Neptune maritime patrol aircraft. Consequently, one of the flanking SHAR two-ships would be dedicated to finding and attacking the low-flying 'SUEs' while the other intercepted the main formation from abeam and attempted to destroy more FAA Daggers, Skyhawks and Canberras before they could reach the Royal Navy ships.

In the event the CAPs were overwhelmed, outflanked or saturated, or intercepts were missed, an additional pair of SHARs – being held 'on alert' on the decks of each of the two carriers – would be launched immediately and vectored directly up the threat axis.

SHAR tactics development began with the establishment of 700A Intensive Flying Trials Unit (IFTU), which embarked in *Hermes* from October 1980 to March 1981. On deck, XZ451, the first production aircraft, sits in its 700A IFTU markings, while trials aircraft XZ450 immediately behind it carries an AIM-9B and XZ439 is seen landing with a CBLS-100 practice bomb carrier on its port wing outer pylon. XZ451 would subsequently be credited with three victories (two claimed by Lt Cdr Ward) while serving with 801 NAS during the 1982 conflict.

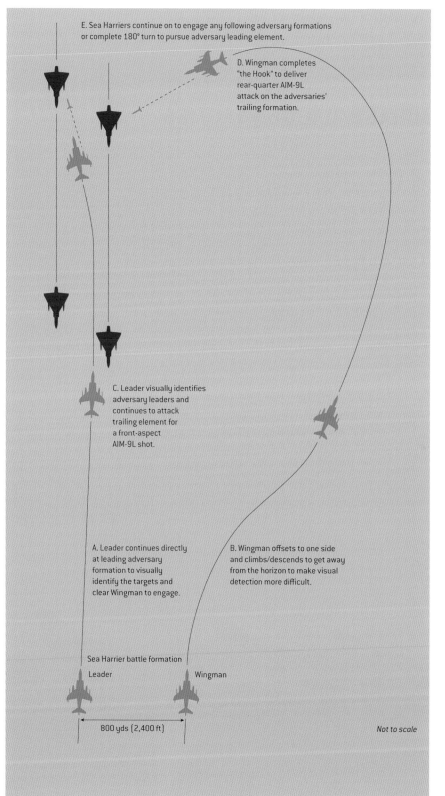

E. Sea Harriers continue on to engage any following adversary formations or complete 180° turn to pursue adversary leading element.

D. Wingman completes "the Hook" to deliver rear-quarter AIM-9L attack on the adversaries' trailing formation.

C. Leader visually identifies adversary leaders and continues to attack trailing element for a front-aspect AIM-9L shot.

A. Leader continues directly at leading adversary formation to visually identify the targets and clear Wingman to engage.

B. Wingman offsets to one side and climbs/descends to get away from the horizon to make visual detection more difficult.

Sea Harrier battle formation

Leader

Wingman

800 yds (2,400 ft)

Not to scale

The Sea Harrier's basic fighting unit was a pair of SHARs that CAPed at an altitude of 12,000–15,000ft, line abreast, with 800 yards between them. This was called 'battle formation'. This arrangement allowed both members of the formation to visually check the other's 'six o'clock' for any aircraft attacking from behind, and permitted both pilots to work their radars without fear of mid-air collision. The typical attack tactic involved one SHAR – usually the leader (#1) – to intercept approaching targets 'head on', while the second (#2) offset to one side to swing round and attack from the rear. One advantage of this attack profile was that, in the event that the approaching targets were not previously identified as enemy aircraft, a VID pass could be flown by the SHAR leader while the wingman 'hooked' round, usually from below, to attack from astern. Called 'the Hook' tactic, it would result in a positive VID before weapons employment, and would wind up with one SHAR being highly offensive and in stern AIM-9 parameters on one, if not both, aircraft in the adversary formation.

41

The intercepts and engagement would continue until the SHARs were 'called off' by the AAWC as the air battle approached the task group's SAM missile engagement zones (MEZ).

MIRAGE/DAGGER TACTICS

Flying an aircraft designed as a supersonic bomber interceptor, Mirage IIIEA pilots typically employed tactics formulated around a two-ship formation that engaged its target(s) following vectoring by GCI. According to veteran Mirage IIIEA pilot Carlos Perona, 'Since ground control [is] guiding the planes, GCI is the one that establishes the best geometry to [engage] until the on-board radar can acquire the targets and, depending on the armament, then the optimal [pursuit] curves to shoot . . . [The] Wingman is fixed [in position] following the commands of the radar that directs the Leader until GCI decides [whether] the best approach [is] to fire head-on with a radar-guided missile, or break to fire from 45° angles with the two planes homing on the target, or finally from "six o'clock".'

Argentine Daggers lacked the Mirage's radar and air-to-air firepower and flew a more defensive formation, with the wingman nearly line abreast of his leader (ten degrees behind the beam) 500 yards to one side, with both jets weaving gently. By doing so they could mutually cover their vulnerable 'six o'clock' while scanning the air for their opponents, relying on GCI radar controllers to position them behind their targets. The leader would then, once he spotted the adversaries, manoeuvre his section to approach the tail of their targets since the Daggers' armament was the very much limited Shafrir-2 IR missile and their 30mm cannon.

For attack missions, Argentine fighter-bombers typically flew in three-ship formations, approaching the target area in a shallow descent that was designed to allow them to remain below the adversary's radar coverage. Lacking RWR, Dagger pilots adopted a formation that would allow them to visually cover each other's 'six o'clock'

Although the Dagger was a dual-role fighter-bomber, Argentine pilots who flew the jet primarily trained for the air-to-ground mission. Approximately 65 per cent of their training sorties were air-to-ground, with the remaining 35 per cent being air-to-air training missions. Here, three *Grupo 6 de Caza*'s *Escuadrón II* Daggers parked on the steel-plate 'alert pad' at BAM San Julián await their next mission against the British task group. (Guillermo Posadas)

– flying almost line-abreast, with the wingmen 200–300 yards on either side of their leader. This allowed them to check the other side of the formation, covering the tails of other two members of the formation. Pilots would turn their heads approximately 135° to each side to scan the area behind the leader and the other wingman while the flight leader focused mainly on navigation to the target.

To remain concealed from enemy radars for as long as possible, and evade SAMs, the target was approached at the lowest possible altitude and very high speed – about 500 knots. Given the speed of the weapons computers aboard Royal Navy warships, it was calculated by the FAA that the target vessel would only be able to lock onto one aircraft at a time before being able to engage the next contact. Therefore, potentially one of the three Daggers would be fired upon, leaving it to try to evade the missile, while the other two would have a less dangerous run to the target.

If multiple targets were presented, the formation would split so that the Daggers attacked up to three targets simultaneously. If only a single target was present, the wingmen would manoeuvre to attack the target in sequence, with sufficient spacing to prevent their own aircraft from being damaged by the bomb blasts of the preceding Dagger.

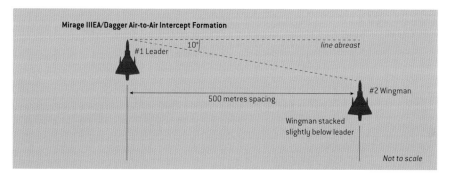

Mirage IIIEA/Dagger Air-to-Air Intercept Formation

#1 Leader — 10° — line abreast

#2 Wingman

500 metres spacing

Wingman stacked slightly below leader

Not to scale

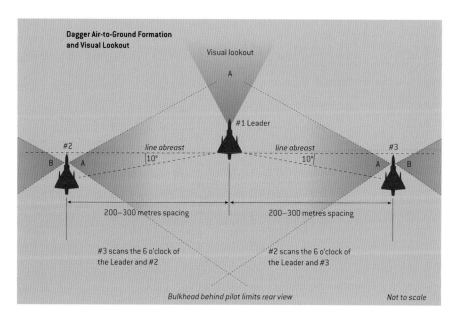

Dagger Air-to-Ground Formation and Visual Lookout

Visual lookout

A

#1 Leader

#2 — line abreast 10° — line abreast 10° — #3

B A A B

200–300 metres spacing   200–300 metres spacing

#3 scans the 6 o'clock of the Leader and #2

#2 scans the 6 o'clock of the Leader and #3

Bulkhead behind pilot limits rear view   Not to scale

The primary Mirage IIIEA combat formation was a two-ship spread formation flown under GCI control. The Leader (#1) followed the GCI instructions while the Wingman (#2) flew about 1,640ft to one side, stacked slightly low, and about ten degrees aft of line abreast. This formation allowed the Leader freedom to manoeuvre the two-ship into proper attack/firing position by following GCI instructions, brought the wingman's radar and weapons to bear on the target as well and at the same time allowed both formation members to visually scan the other's 'six o'clock' for any attackers coming from behind.

During air-to-ground attack missions, Argentine fighter-bombers typically flew three-ship formations, with the Leader (#1) navigating to the target and the Wingmen (#2 and #3) being responsible for the defensive lookout. Therefore, the Leader's primary scan was straight ahead, +/-30° off his nose, to ensure none of the formation members hit any obstacles ahead. The Wingman's primary visual lookout (A) was from the lead aircraft aft, scanning for adversaries making stern attacks on the opposite side of the formation or the leader. The Wingman's secondary responsibility (B) was to scan outside the formation for adversaries coming in on beam attacks from his side of the formation since that might be beyond the visual range of the opposite wingman.

43

DAVID A. B. SMITH

Born in Lustleigh, Devon, on 9 April 1955, David A. B. Smith joined the Royal Navy as a General List Seaman Officer at the age of 18 in September 1973. While he was undergoing his initial training at the Britannia Royal Naval College at Dartmouth, several of Smith's peers expressed an interest in specialising in aviation and, although he originally had no interest in flying, he eventually decided that this would be his preferred career path.

After a period at sea as a midshipman in the Leander-class frigate HMS *Ariadne*, and then as a sub-lieutenant navigating the North Sea offshore patrol vessel HMS *Jersey*, Smith began flying training on the Scottish Aviation Bulldog T 1 at the Royal Naval Elementary Flying Training School at RAF Leeming, in Yorkshire, in September 1978. His natural talent and rapidly developing skills resulted in his selection for fast jet training, so Smith was seconded to the RAF for basic, advanced and weapons training courses and, finally, was introduced to the Harrier GR 3 in the summer of 1981. Returning to the Royal Navy to complete the Operational Flying Training course on the Sea Harrier FRS 1 at RNAS Yeovilton, he qualified for frontline service in early 1982.

Assigned to 800 NAS, Smith embarked for the first time in HMS *Hermes* in March 1982, which deployed to the South Atlantic early the next month. During the Falklands/Malvinas conflict he was mentioned in dispatches for his actions during a number of air combat sorties over the islands, particularly on the occasion when he and his flight leader, Lt Cdr Andy Auld, intercepted and destroyed a three-ship of FAA Dagger fighter-bombers.

In 1984 he was appointed as the Commanding Officer of the *Ton*-class minesweeper, HMS *Beachampton*, based in Hong Kong, before returning as a tactical instructor to the Sea Harrier training squadron, 899 NAS, based at RNAS Yeovilton in 1986. The next year he began his final appointment as Senior Pilot and second-in-command of 800 NAS embarked in HMS *Illustrious*, before resigning his Royal Navy commission in early 1989. Smith subsequently joined Cathay Pacific Airways and is now a Senior Captain, having flown the Airbus A330 and, more recently, the new Airbus A350-900. He is married and lives with his wife, Sharon, in the New Territories, Hong Kong.

Lt David A. B. Smith, upon his return to Yeovilton from the South Atlantic in the summer of 1982. (David Smith)

GUILLERMO ADOLFO DONADILLE

Guillermo Adolfo Donadille was born in Pigüé, a small French immigrant town south of Buenos Aires, on 17 February 1948. Being an avid reader, as a child he marvelled at the progress made by the Argentine aviation industry during the early 1950s, especially when the first indigenous jet fighters – the Fábrica Militar de Aviones IAe 27/33 Pulqui I and II – were developed. At 16 years of age, he was accepted into the *Escuela de Aviación Militar* (Military Aviation Academy), becoming an *Alférez* (ensign, or acting pilot officer) in December 1967. Having passed the FAA's screening flying gliders, Donadille began training to become a military pilot, 'winning his wings' one year later following approximately 130 hours in the FMA-built T-34A Mentor.

Posted next to the *Escuela de Caza de la Fuerza Aérea Argentina* (Air Force Fighter School), he received another 100 hours flying the armed Morane-Saulnier MS.760 Paris. Following fighter pilot training, Donadille was posted to *Grupo 5 de Caza*, where he flew the A-4B Skyhawk, becoming an instructor and amassing 500 hours on the light attack jet. Consequently, he was well qualified to be one of the original Dagger pilots and, in 1978, was sent to Israel for training. By January 1982 Donadille had accumulated 600 hours in the new high-performance fighter-bomber and, obviously a rising star, was sent to study at the *Escuela Superior de Guerra Aérea* (Air War College). On 3 April, the day after Argentina repossessed the islands, Donadille requested a return to *Grupo 6 de Caza*. He participated in combat on 1 May, but on his second mission, on 21 May, he was shot down by a Sea Harrier CAP while en route to his target.

Continuing his career after the war, Donadille was placed in charge of activating '*Escuadron 55*' in 1984, the unit being equipped with ex-IDF/AF Mirage IIICJs and named after the 55 FAA members that lost their lives during the conflict. He subsequently commanded *Grupo 6 de Caza* and later *VI Brigada Aérea* at Tandil. Overall, in his 40-year career, Donadille logged more than 6,000 flight hours as a military pilot, including 1,000+ hours in the Mirage and Dagger. He retired in 2003 as brigadier major (two-star general) and currently serves as an advisor for a Province of Córdoba Legislator.

Capt Guillermo 'Poncho' Donadille (left), with his crewchief and Dagger C-407. (Guillermo Donadille)

COMBAT

The fighting over the Falklands/Malvinas started with a 'bang' – actually 21 of them – on 1 May when, at 0446hrs (local time), that number of 1,000lb general purpose bombs rained upon Stanley airfield/BAM Malvinas from a solitary Avro Vulcan bomber (XM607 from No. 44 Sqn, codenamed 'Black Buck 1'); one bomb hit the runway but did not affect its operability. In response Brigadier Crespo launched a pair of *Grupo 8 de Caza* Mirages IIIEAs – each carrying a pair of Matra R 550 Magics and two 1,700-litre (375 gal) drop tanks – from BAM Río Gallegos. Led by the squadron commander, Maj José Sánchez, 'Fiera' flight arrived 'on station' at around 0730hrs, but could not make radio contact with Radar Malvinas and shortly thereafter returned to base.

As the skies began lightening in the east, TG 317.8 approached East Falkland/Isla Soledad from the northeast. At 0600hrs (Local (L) Time on the Falkland Islands/Islas Malvinas was the same as Buenos Aires time, three hours earlier than GMT/Zulu (Z) Time and four hours earlier than British Summer Time (GMT+1), so 0600L was 0900Z), *Invincible* began launching four Sea Harriers to establish two CAP orbits east and northeast of Port Stanley/Puerto Argentino, being controlled by the *County*-class destroyer HMS *Glamorgan*. After being on station for an hour, the jets were replaced by two more pairs of SHARs, the original group refuelling and returning an hour later – this routine meant that continuous CAP coverage was provided for the warships as they approached a position about 90nm northeast of Port Stanley.

From *Hermes*, 12 more SHARs commenced taking off at 0748hrs, forming three attack groups flying at low level towards the island's northeast shore. Making landfall 20nm north of the primary target – Stanley airfield/BAM Malvinas – 'Red Section' headed southwest to attack the airfield's AAA defences from the north while the main force, 'Black Section' led by Lt Cdr Andy Auld (in XZ494), swung round to attack from the northwest. Finally, 'Tartan Section' followed the island's north coast, then flew down Falkland Sound/Estrecho de San Carlos to attack the grass airfield at Goose Green, called BAM Cóndor by the Argentines.

About this time, 'Toro' flight – a pair of Daggers flown by Capitán (Capt) Carlos 'Talo' Moreno (in C-437) and Teniente (Lt) Héctor 'Lince' Volponi (in C-430) from *Grupo 6 de Caza's Escuadrón II* at BAN Río Grande – crossed Estrecho de San Carlos at an altitude in excess of 30,000ft and checked in with Radar Malvinas.

Each jet was carrying a pair of Shafrir-2s and three 1,300-litre (285 gal) drop tanks. The GCI radar could not see the attackers speeding inbound at low level, but it had detected the SHAR CAPs at 15,000ft and vectored Moreno's Daggers on a 030° heading to engage the northern pair of British jets. This CAP was manned by Lt Cdr Robin Kent (in ZA175) and Lt Brian Haigh (in XZ498), who were vectored by *Glamorgan's* Fighter Direction Officer (FDO) on a reciprocal heading to intercept them.

At the merge (where the two radar plots become one on the GCI scopes) 'Toro' flight began circling to the right, visually searching desperately for the SHARs about 4,000ft below them and, failing to find them, headed home low on fuel. Kent and Haigh also never spotted their adversaries, although they did see the Daggers' jettisoned fuel tanks, streaming excess fuel, falling through the air and reported them as AAMs fired out of range. In any event, neither side fired any weapons at the other and both returned to base without having seen their opponents.

About the time 'Toro' flight was vectored against the northern CAP, at 0823hrs BAM Malvinas was attacked by five Sea Harriers that dropped 18 BL755 cluster bomb units (CBUs) on parked aircraft and other soft targets and three Mk 17 delay/retard 1,000lb HEMC bombs on the runway. The fuel dump and the maintenance hangar were hit – both going up in flames – but the runway was not appreciably damaged. Meanwhile, three other SHARs attacked Goose Green/BAM Cóndor with CBUs and delay-action Mk 17s, one bomb hitting the grass runway. The raid destroyed an IA.58 Pucará (*Grupo 3 de Ataque*) light attack aircraft, killing the pilot as he attempted to dive out of the cockpit, as well as eight mechanics, wounding seven more. Only one SHAR was slightly damaged by AAA fire, with all of them recovering safely aboard *Hermes*. Here, the underwing bomb racks were exchanged for LAU-7A/5 missile launcher rails that were quickly loaded with AIM-9Ls. After the conversion to air-to-air configuration, 800 NAS began taking its turn manning the CAPs, which now included a third one southeast of Port Stanley.

The airfield attacks were followed shortly by Radar Malvinas reporting possible landing craft approaching from the east. CdoFAS immediately organised two 'armed reconnaissance' maritime strike missions using eight A-4B/C Skyhawks carrying 250kg (550lb) bombs. The first mission ('Topo' flight – four *Grupo 5 de Caza* A-4Bs) launched from BAM Río Gallegos, covered by two Mirages – 'Tablón' flight, flown by Capt Gustavo Argentino 'Paco' García Cuerva (in I-019) and Primer Teniente (1Lt) Carlos 'Daga' Perona (in I-015). The latter pilots took off from the same airfield as the

Combat operations began before dawn on 1 May when 801 NAS launched four SHARs to man two CAPs to cover the approach of 800 NAS's 12 SHARs headed inbound to attack Stanley airport/BAM Malvinas and Goose Green airfield/BAM Cóndor.

A-4s some 29 minutes later, and, using their greater speed, rapidly closed up behind the Skyhawks as the attack aircraft approached the islands. Radar Malvinas duly paired Capt Hugo Palaver's 'Topo' flight – mistaking them for 'Tablón' flight – against the northern SHAR CAP, which was manned by Lt Cdr John 'E J' Eyton-Jones (XZ456) and Flt Lt Paul Barton (XZ493). Barton later stated, 'I remember the controller saying, "I've got trade for you – two bandits closing from the west, range 120 miles", and he gave us a vector towards them. Then he said, "Er, 15 miles astern of them are two more – another raid – strength two. Er . . . er . . . there's two more behind them . . ." He was a very inexperienced young sub-lieutenant, and with each call his voice was getting higher and higher.'

Meanwhile, Garcia Cuerva recognised Radar Malvinas's mistake and, after some confusion, corrected the GCI controller, who ordered 'Topo' flight to withdraw. Due to the large altitude difference between the CAP at 15,000ft and the Skyhawks, the SHAR pilots never obtained a radar contact and, only two nautical miles from 'the merge', Palaver turned tail to the Sea Harriers.

Unable to spot the Skyhawks due to a layer of high cloud above them, Eyton-Jones led his flight back to the CAP, now pursued by García Cuerva and Perona. As the latter later recalled, 'We accomplished our aim because when the [SHAR] CAP realised we were behind them, they changed course to face us. We separated ourselves by between 1,000 and 2,000m [3,280 to 6,560ft] to try a shot from the front with our R 530 missiles, but the radars didn't provide good illumination and because of our low fuel we headed back to Río Gallegos. We landed at 1058[hrs], thinking we would not make it since I only had 240 litres [50 gal] of fuel and my boss only 200 [45 gal] when we landed.'

During the mission debrief – and preparing for their afternoon sorties – Perona recalled García Cuerva being particularly keen to engage the Sea Harriers next time, adding that his flight leader said, 'If [we get] low on fuel we'll try to land in Puerto Argentino [Port Stanley], refuel in Alfa config[uration – clean, i.e., remove tanks and missiles], and return to the continent.'

A series of feints flown by Royal Navy Sea King helicopters around midday convinced Menéndez that the British were inserting special forces in anticipation of an amphibious operation. This led CdoFAS to launch three pairs of Shafrir-2-armed A-4Cs (*Grupo 4 de Caza*) on staggered anti-helicopter sweeps of the island, covered by

CdoFAS's response to the 'Black Buck' Vulcan bombing mission was to send relays of Matra-armed Mirage IIIEAs and Shafrir-2-carrying Daggers over the contested islands, resulting in several inconclusive engagements on 1 May. (Jorge Fazio)

two flights of Daggers – 'Fierro' flight swept ahead and 'Ciclón' flight provided egress coverage. Additionally, Brigadier Castellano ordered three of the four T-34C-1 Turbo-Mentors from BAN Calderón (airstrip on Pebble Island/Isla Borbón) to take off at 1225hrs and hunt down the Royal Navy helicopters.

Meanwhile, 'Blue 1' flight – two 801 NAS SHARs flown by Ward (in XZ495) and Lt Mike 'Soapy' Watson (in ZA175) – established a CAP about 20nm northeast of Stanley at 12,000ft, covering the frigates *Brilliant* and *Yarmouth*, which were conducting ASW operations north of Cape Bougainville. As Ward later explained, 'The anti-submarine operation was only about 20 miles west of our CAP station, so we were in a good position to provide assistance if needed. [Then] *Glamorgan* suddenly called us up. "I have two, no, three contacts slow moving, departing Stanley [*sic*] and turning up the coast to the north." Our battle pair rounded to the south and commenced descent.'

In the first engagement between SHARs and Argentine aircraft in which shots were fired, Lt Mike 'Soapy' Watson led his 801 NAS CO, Lt Cdr Nigel 'Sharkey' Ward, to intercept three COAN T-34C-1 Turbo-Mentors that were stalking a Royal Navy Sea King helicopter. Watson's over-land 'look down' radar intercept was an exceptional feat using the Blue Fox pulse radar. (Mike Watson)

In a remarkable feat, looking with his Blue Fox angled downwards, Watson detected the targets six nautical miles away, 20 degrees to the right. He later recalled, 'I got them on radar – and we whizzed down through about 8/10ths of cloud with the base at about 2,000ft and a bit murky beneath in light rain. We came out of the cloud at about 450kt in a good position about a mile and a half in their "four o'clock". They saw us straight away and they jettisoned whatever ordnance they were carrying and hot footed it up into the murk.'

In fact, the three T-34Cs were stalking a Sea King HAS 5 of 826 NAS that was weaving through the terrain attempting to evade their attack. One of the pilots (Teniente de Fragata Miguel Uberti) spotted the SHARs and called 'Harrier, Harrier! Two on our tail!' The Turbo-Mentors jettisoned their 70mm rocket and 7.62mm gun pods and climbed briskly into cloud, but not before Ward put a 30mm round through one of their rear canopies.

Watson continued, 'On completion of that "intercept" we were given two bogeys south[west] at about 50 miles closing, fast, high. Great – we were climbing up through about 10,000ft and felt a bit vulnerable! We faced up [turned towards the threat] and they turned about so we went back to CAP. They then turned in again and repeated the performance. We went back to CAP, struggling to get some height and speed. They turned in again. Sharkey said "let's keep going cold [pointing away from the threat – 'hot' is nose-on to the threat] until they have to commit", which we did. We turned hot (we were at about 20,000ft at this time) and they were at about 20 miles, coming down the hill from high level at high speed. They fired a pair of Matra 530s at us – we saw the trails – and although we had no RWR indications, we thought it best to break left to avoid! The Mirages/Daggers blew through at high-speed and bugged out to the west.'

The two SHARs had in fact duelled with a single Dagger, flown by Capt Raúl 'Tigre' Díaz (in C-421), whose wingman had aborted due to engine problems. Díaz recalled, 'Close to the islands, I made contact with CIC at Puerto Argentino, who directed me towards a contact at 60 miles, east of the islands. I armed the missile and gun panel and turned to a [heading] of 090°, following the CIC's instructions. They told me the intruder was 6,000ft below. The controller continued indicating [bearing] and distance, and we were closing head-on [but at 12 miles] the radar lost it. The radar operator made me return to the west . . . Then he alerted me about a [radar] return flying towards me, very fast and climbing. It was detected 18 miles from me and I turned onto a collision [intercept] course, keeping a height of 26,000ft and accelerating to 450 knots. When I was just eight miles from the intruders and 3,000ft above them, they decided to abandon the engagement. They descended rapidly until our radar [controller] lost them.'

That afternoon *Glamorgan* and the frigates *Alacrity* and *Arrow* were detached from the main body of TG 317.8 to follow up the morning's airfield attacks with a naval bombardment. At 1425hrs the three warships arrived nine nautical miles offshore and began shelling BAM Malvinas. Thirty-five minutes later, amid the din of crashing 4.5in shells, Radar Malvinas detected what was thought to be five landing craft 13nm to the east, approaching. Believing the anticipated British amphibious assault had begun, Menéndez reported to TOAS that a 'landing by helicopter in the northern sector of the islands, supported by logistics vessels or the carrier, is in progress. The ships are positioned on a radius between 010° and 145° off Puerto Argentino at 90, 40 and 10nm. Sea Harriers are providing cover for helicopter landings.'

Immediately, Crespo ordered maximum effort maritime strikes against the British ships. Six Canberra B 62 bomber sorties were organised by *Grupo 2 de Bombardeo* at Trelew, while *Grupos 4* and *5 de Caza* launched 12 Skyhawks and *Grupo 6 de Caza's Escuadrón II* contributed three bomb-armed Daggers. These 21 strikers would be covered by two pairs of *Grupo 8 de Caza* Mirages sweeping ahead of the first attackers, followed by four *Grupo 6* Daggers – two from each squadron – to cover their egress.

The two sections of Magic-armed Mirages began taking off from BAM Río Gallegos at 1545hrs. 'Dardo' section – flown by García Cuerva (I-015) and Perona (I-019) – were followed five minutes later by 'Buitre' section. Also at 1545hrs, 'Torno Flight' – the three *Escuadrón II* Daggers, each carrying a pair of 250kg (550lb) parachute-retarded BRP-250 bombs – roared off from BAM San Julián, followed 15 minutes later by 'Fortín' section, which was to provide egress top cover for the fighter-bombers. To provide additional egress coverage, at 1554hrs *Escuadrón III* at BAN Río Grande launched a single Shafrir-2-armed Dagger – 'Rubio 2' (C-433), flown by 1Lt Jose 'Pepe' Ardiles. 'Rubio 1' had ground aborted due to a maintenance problem. This set the stage for the decisive clashes of the day.

Leading the fighter sweep, 'Dardo' section entered from the west at 35,000ft, and at 1625hrs Radar Malvinas vectored them against the Royal Navy's northern CAP. As Perona later recalled, 'The radar operator decided to separate us to intercept the CAP, so we turned 45 degrees to each side of the heading we were on. Then we jettisoned the 1,700 [litre (375 gal)] external tanks we were carrying, but a failure on my plane led to only one being released – the right tank remained in place. Then the operator ordered another course change and told me I had a target 30 miles ahead on the opposite heading and lower than me, so I started a gentle dive.'

Capt Gustavo Argentino 'Paco' García Cuerva after soloing in Mirage IIIEA I-007 in 1978. (Gabriel Fioni)

Glamorgan's Type 965 radar detected the pair of Mirages at a range of approximately 120nm and, as they approached, the ship's FDO alerted the CAP – manned by 801 NAS's Flt Lt Paul Barton (on an exchange tour from the RAF, flying XZ452) and Lt Steve Thomas (in XZ453) – and at 40nm vectored them towards the 'bogeys'. They pushed over, descending to 11,000ft and accelerating to 400 knots to meet the fast-approaching threat.

Thomas got the first radar contact and Barton quickly passed him the leader's role, calling for a 'hook' attack. Pointing at the Mirages, Thomas began a slight climb, later stating, 'We were running in towards each other, head-on. I was doing 400 knots . . . I locked my radar on to their leader, then I began looking for the others [*sic*] . . . I got a visual at about eight miles and saw it was a Mirage. And I could also see his No. 2, just to the right and behind. I was trying to lock a Sidewinder on him but the missile would not "acquire". I didn't get any growl so I couldn't fire it.'

Perona explained, 'Radar Malvinas told me [the target] was only ten miles away, and because I didn't have it on my radar, I made a visual search. I saw it in contrast with the clouds below, and when I was about six or seven miles away I confirmed that I had a Sea Harrier, on an opposite course.' Angling in from their individual vectors, García Cuerva and Perona's formation collapsed into a more traditional 'fighting wing' arrangement, with both descending towards Thomas, while Barton dived away, accelerating even more – to 550 knots – and swung wide to the right to get 'turning room' so that he could attack from behind.

Later, Barton recalled, 'I accelerated to maximum speed and eased right to get displacement, locking my radar on to the No. 2 as I did so. I dived down, visually acquiring the bogeys at about five miles. I was relieved to see them visually – the eye is much better at comprehending three-dimensional information and I really did not look at the radar again . . . The leader came across my [nose] from right to left at about two and a half miles, and as he did so [he] began a very gentle port turn.'

Thomas met the two Mirages head-on, later explaining, 'I began turning hard to the right, and passed about 100ft above the top of their leader. I could make out every detail of the aircraft, its camouflage pattern, and see the pilot in his cockpit.' Continuing his hard right turn, Thomas passed over Perona's Mirage almost immediately afterwards, crossing his 'six o'clock' as the Argentine pilot initiated his own manoeuvre.

Perona explained, 'Before crossing with [the Sea Harrier] I began a steep climb to gain height, but the tank I was still carrying reduced my climb performance, and when I looked to one side I clearly saw the Sea Harrier climbing to my left, about 500m [1640ft] away, so we entered a scissors manoeuvre, gaining a separation of only 100–200m [330–655ft]. I followed the [Sea] Harrier until it disappeared from my field of view through the top aft side of my cockpit canopy.'

As the two opponents began a vertical scissors, unseen from below and left, Barton curved upwards to engage the trailing Mirage, shedding knots rapidly in the 6g climbing turn. He stated, 'I held the turn, still keeping him [Perona] and his leader in view through the top of my canopy. As I continued into his "six" the 'winder began to growl as it got its lock angle. This was a welcome noise because it confirmed my chance to get him and he was now outside gun range and separating fast. I completed the turn and was on his tail at about 500 yards. I was doing about 350kt, but he was going about 150kt faster and began to pull away. I was aware that he was faster than

I was, but with the 'winder locked up and well within range, I [fired] . . . At first I thought it had failed. It came off the rail and ducked down . . . It took about half a mile for it to get its trajectory sorted out, then it picked itself up and for the last half mile just homed straight in. The missile flight time was about four seconds, and then the missile hit him on the port side of the fuselage, then the whole rear half of the aircraft disappeared in a great ball of flame. The front half went down burning fiercely, arcing [downwards] towards the sea.'

Looking over his left shoulder, García Cuerva had seen the approaching missile and shouted for Perona to 'break', but it was too late. Perona recalled, 'Just as I was starting to manoeuvre to eyeball the Sea Harrier again, I felt a big jolt. My Mirage started to shudder badly and I lost control, and the warning lights of the panel illuminated in quick succession. After futile attempts to control my machine, I ejected.' Fighting for control, Perona shut down the burning Atar turbojet and pointed the Mirage south, gliding towards land, but when the jet began rolling to the right and would not respond to his control inputs, he ejected, descending onto the shore of Pebble Island/ Isla Borbón. Breaking a foot in the landing, Perona was rescued later that day.

Now García Cuerva saw that he was 1-vs-2 and immediately went into a hard slicing defensive turn, spiralling downwards into the cloud deck 8,000ft below. This gave Thomas plenty of vertical turning room and he followed, stating later, 'I rolled into a vertical descent behind him, locked on one of my missiles and fired it. The missile streaked after him and just before he reached the cloud I saw it pass close to his tail. Then both the aircraft and the missile vanished [into cloud].'

Thomas followed through the undercast searching for evidence that his target had crashed, but there was none. He returned to *Invincible* to report one Mirage 'possibly destroyed'. Undamaged, but now low on both fuel and altitude, García Cuerva decided to land at Stanley Airport/BAM Malvinas. Tragically, he was shot down and killed by the airfield's 30mm AAA gunners.

The year after the conflict, an otherwise authoritative history reported that the reason García Cuerva headed for BAM Malvinas was that Thomas's Sidewinder detonated 'close to the enemy fighter and caused considerable damage. Streaming fuel from his punctured tanks, Cuerva . . . headed for Port Stanley to try to bring his crippled aircraft down on the runway there.' The book's authors claimed to have 'confirmed' Thomas's 'kill'. Actually, post-conflict recovery of wreckage of I-015 from the shallow waters around Maggie Elliot Rock, just south of the airfield, revealed no evidence of AIM-9 damage.

After diving into the undercast to escape the heat-seeking missile, it was apparent that García Cuerva did not have enough fuel to climb back to altitude and return to BAM Río Gallegos, so – just as he

Following the opening airfield attacks on 1 May, both SHAR NASs repeatedly launched pairs of jets to man two of the three CAP orbits protecting helicopter-borne flight operations and an ongoing ASW prosecution. (Nigel 'Sharkey' Ward)

had said to Perona in the mission briefing – he attempted to land at the island's airport instead. Thomas did not learn the fate of his adversary until after the conflict, and was awarded the 'kill' based on the confounded logic that 'because, even had it landed, [the aircraft] would probably never have been able to take off again'.

As the brief air battle between the SHARS and the Mirage IIIEAs raged overhead, the three Dagger fighter-bombers of 'Torno' flight – led by Capt Norberto Rubén 'Joker' Dimeglio (in C-432), with 1Lt César 'Zorro' Román (C-407) and Lt Gustavo Aguirre 'Boxer' Faget (C-412) on his wing – raced at 420 knots across the waves north of West Falkland/Gran Malvina heading east at an altitude of 50ft. Dimeglio had led his three-ship strike formation down through the undercast while over the Jason Islands/Islas Sebaldes. While the islands' terrain masked 'Torno' flight from *Glamorgan*'s radars, they were intermittently detected by *Invincible*'s much better Type 1022 radar. With Barton and Thomas's CAP engaging the Mirages over Pebble Island/Isla Bórbon, *Invincible* quickly scrambled 801 NAS's 'alert pair' to deal with what was perceived as a raid coming directly at the main body of TG 317.8.

Post-conflict examination of the wreckage of García Cuerva's Mirage IIIEA revealed two errors in previous written histories of the conflict. The aircraft was 'I-015' rather than the previously accepted 'I-019' and there was no evidence of damage from Lt Steve Thomas's AIM-9L. (Allan White)

Meanwhile, as one of the day's veterans recalled, 'On the CIC frequency, all of us, Torno and Fortín flights, could hear García and Perona yelling instructions at each other as they engaged the Sea Harriers.' Passing along the north shore of Pebble Island/Isla Borbón, 'Torno 2' – Lt Faget – spotted Thomas's SHAR to the south, circling beneath the grey overcast, and called out 'Attention! Harrier at "three o'clock"!' The SHAR quickly disappeared, Thomas making a climbing turn back into cloud to rejoin Barton above and return to *Invincible*.

Finding nothing off the north coast, Dimeglio led his formation – flying nearly line abreast with 165ft between each – around Cape Carysfort/Cabo Corrientes on East Falkland/Isla Soledad's northeastern end and, accelerating to 480 knots, headed south looking for warships reported to be 15nm northeast of Port Stanley/Puerto Argentino. At 1637hrs he spotted the three British ships five nautical miles offshore to the southeast and immediately called for individual attacks.

As 'Torno 3', Román later explained, 'We arrived in the target zone but nothing was there, so we continued to Puerto Argentino. We could see that something was firing against coastal positions, and ahead of us we saw explosions like fireworks. Then we saw them, three frigates [*sic*] very close to Puerto Argentino and constantly firing. I heard our leader saying, "No. 1 [will take] the ship in the middle, No. 2 the one on the left and 3 the one to the right!" We flew as low as we could, over a calm and grey sea, under a low cloud base at no more than 1,000ft. We went full throttle for the attack . . . AAA fire was very light and I think we caught them off guard. I dropped the two 250kg [550lb] parachute-retarded bombs into "my" ship and [began] taking evasive action.'

The three Daggers completely surprised the warships – only *Glamorgan* responded, firing its 20mm Oerlikon cannon at the attackers – and 'popped up', one of them as high as 3,000ft, for shallow dive-bomb deliveries and strafing passes with their 30mm cannon. In the first-ever anti-ship attacks flown by FAA pilots, the bombs narrowly

missed, the underwater shocks splitting seams in *Alacrity*'s hull and 'dishing' plates on *Glamorgan*'s. *Arrow* was hit by 11 30mm shells, causing impressive but superficial damage to its funnel and engine air intake – one sailor was wounded.

Almost simultaneously, flying into the combat zone from the southwest was 'Rubio 2', a single Dagger (C-433) piloted by 1Lt Jose 'Pepe' Ardiles. After checking in with Radar Malvinas, he was vectored against what initially appeared to be a single contact approaching from the northeast. This single contact was actually 800 NAS's CAP, stationed southeast of Port Stanley/Puerto Argentino, the pair of SHARs being flown by Lt Martin Hale (believed to have been flying XZ460) and Flt Lt Tony 'Bertie' Penfold (in XZ455). With *Glamorgan* working the 801 NAS CAP against 'Dardo Section' and *Invincible* busy directing its 'alert jets' against the intermittent contact ('Torno' flight) that had disappeared at low level, *Hermes* took control of this pair and vectored them against the inbound Dagger.

Approaching head-on, with the SHARs climbing through 20,000ft, Hale had the lead because Penfold's Blue Fox was unserviceable. Hale was busying himself attempting a radar lock-on when, at a range of eight nautical miles, Penfold visually acquired their adversary, calling, 'Targets at "12 o'clock high"'. Seconds later, Ardiles spotted Hale's jet at seven nautical miles and reportedly fired a Shafrir-2 (although this may have been another instance of British pilots mistaking jettisoned external fuel tanks for missile firings), well outside its envelope. Suspecting it was an R 530E radar missile, Hale broke hard downhill, slicing towards the clouds, bottoming out at 5,000ft as the 'missile' went ballistic and disappeared into the undercast.

Alerted at the last moment that two SHARs were present, Ardiles immediately went into a hard climbing turn in full reheat – in front of Penfold – but was unable to escape. With the '9-Lima' growling angrily in his headset, Penfold unleashed the missile inside three nautical miles. By the time it shot across this distance, Ardiles had completed the 180° turn. The missile ran up the Dagger's tailpipe and detonated, shredding the Argentine jet. It erupted into a fireball and fell in pieces into Choiseul Sound/Seno Choiseul and Lively Island/Isla Bougainville at 1640hrs. Lt Ardiles did not survive.

Following their attack against the three British warships, 'Torno' flight broke right in full reheat and roared off to the northwest, crossing East Falkland/Isla Soledad supersonic at low level, egressing separately and, in and out of the low clouds, losing sight of one another. Passing Estrecho de San Carlos, Dimeglio called for a climb to save fuel. 'Torno 1' zoomed to 42,000ft and 'Torno 3' to 30,000ft, while 'Torno 2' lagged behind at 21,000ft, all of them jettisoning their empty ventral fuel tanks to reduce drag. Román recalled, 'We flew through the clouds and lost each other in the climb. We were returning individually. Then we heard the radar operator saying, "Tornos! You have bandits on your tail!"'

Meanwhile, orbiting over the south end of Falkland Sound at 30,000ft to cover 'Torno' flight's egress was 'Fortín', a two-ship section flown by Capt Guillermo 'Poncho' Donadille (in C-403) and 1Lt Jorge 'Daga' Senn (in C-421). When Donadille called for a 'weapons check' he discovered that an electrical fault had disabled his 30mm DEFA cannon. However, his Shafrir-2 missiles seemed unaffected. While the two Daggers were circling, Radar Malvinas reported that bandits were chasing 'Torno 2' 16nm to the northwest. This was 801 NAS's recently scrambled 'alert pair'. Learning that *Glamorgan*'s task unit had been attacked, *Invincible* sent them after the three attackers, which were climbing at high speed westwards, but the subsonic SHARs were hopelessly behind in an eight-nautical mile tail chase. The Sea Harriers locked onto 'Torno 2', but even at full power the SHARs closed agonisingly slowly.

Eager to engage despite his disabled guns, Donadille turned his two-ship onto a 320° heading. They jettisoned their drop tanks, lit their afterburners – accelerating to Mach 1.4 – and raced to the rescue. Crossing West Falkland/Gran Malvina, the SHARs got within three nautical miles of 'Torno 2' as 'Fortín' flight in turn closed to within two nautical miles of the pair of Sea Harriers. However, without radar, and looking directly into the bright late afternoon sun, the two Argentine pilots of 'Fortín' flight could not locate their prey. Unable to visually acquire the SHARs due to the sun's glare, Donadille controlled his closure to ensure he and Senn did not 'fly out in front' of the British jets. After a fruitless 70nm pursuit, the Sea Harriers gave up. 'Fortín Flight' spotted the Sea Harriers as they sliced down to the left, but, also low on fuel, declined to follow.

The conflict's first coordinated attack against Royal Navy surface units, using Mirage IIIEAs and Daggers to provide pre-strike sweep and post-strike egress coverage, was over. A tactical success – 'Torno' flight was able to ingress and attack its target unimpeded by the SHARs – it came at great expense. Two Mirage IIIEAs and a Dagger had been lost.

The first encounter between Sea Harriers and Mirage IIIEAs was decisive. To engage, the Mirage pilots had had to descend into their adversary's operating envelope, but in doing so they were completely outclassed by the SHAR pilots' employment of the all-aspect AIM-9L. With the loss of one third of its more capable second batch of Mirages, CdoFAS immediately decided that its most sophisticated interceptor was not suited to the air superiority role after all. *Grupo 8 de Caza* would subsequently fly a further 35 combat sorties during the conflict, but they were limited to high-altitude sweeps and decoying feints, intercept attempts

'Torno' flight – Román, Dimeglio, and Faget – following their attack on *Glamorgan* and the frigates *Arrow* and *Alacrity*. (Exequiel Martinez)

against suspected clandestine British helicopter operations and escort of Canberra night bombing missions.

Meanwhile, both Dagger squadrons were committed to low altitude, high-speed maritime strikes in the hope that speed alone would be an effective antidote to the deadly SHAR/AIM-9L combination. By the same token, the two SHAR squadrons – as well as the Task Group's FDOs – realised that high altitude, high-speed intruders could be safely ignored, allowing the SHAR pilots to concentrate on intercepting targets approaching at low altitude.

This proved to be the case within an hour of the day's decisive air battle, when two formations, each consisting of three Canberra B 62s, approached TG 317.8 from the northwest. The first, 'Ruta' flight, encountered the ASW task unit at 1715hrs and the leading bomber (B-105) was damaged while dodging a perceived SAM launch by *Brilliant*, forcing the flight to abandon its mission.

Following 15 minutes later was 'Rifle' flight, which was detected descending from 30,000ft at 120nm by *Invincible*. The carrier's next CAP – flown by Lt Cdr Mike Broadwater (in ZA175) and Lt Alan Curtis (in XZ451) – was vectored towards the threat as it disappeared at low level. In a classic, well-executed low altitude intercept, the SHARs and their pilots performed nearly flawlessly. Curtis fired both his AIM-9Ls and downed one Canberra (B-110) – both crewmen ejected but did not survive. The other two bombers jettisoned their ordnance and wingtip tanks and escaped.

The three-week period between Britain's initial challenge to Argentina's possession of the Falkland Islands/Islas Malvinas and the Royal Navy's amphibious TG 317.0 actually showing up to do something about it was blighted by extremely poor weather that permitted only occasional clashes between the opposing forces. After thwarting the Argentine Navy's attempt to engage TG 317.8 in an air-surface action, Admiral Woodward closed on the islands again on 4 May to deliver additional airfield attacks. One 800 NAS Sea Harrier (XZ459) and its pilot, Lt Nick Taylor, were lost to 35mm AAA fire during the attack on Goose Green/BAM Cóndor.

That same day two COAN Super Étendards from *2da Escuadrilla de Caza y Ataque* destroyed the Type 42 destroyer HMS *Sheffield* with an Exocet missile. Two 801 NAS CAPs were on station, but one (Kent and Haigh) 'were told to investigate but found nothing' and the second (Eyton-Jones and Barton) was ordered off CAP to 'carry out a visual search for enemy surface units' 120nm southwest of the fleet. Under similar instructions, two days later, two 801 NAS SHARs were lost when Eyton-Jones (in XZ452) and Curtis (in XZ453) apparently collided in cloud or hit the water while descending to investigate 'a small surface contact'.

On the Argentine side, after the initial aerial battles, it fell upon the Daggers and Skyhawks to continue the maritime air campaign without direct air coverage. However, because the FAA lacked a maritime reconnaissance capability for locating ships at sea, they would have to wait until TG 317.0 arrived to conduct its amphibious operation. This happened just before midnight on 20 May, when three waves of vessels – two large assault ships (LPDs), five smaller landing ships (LSLs), two RFA replenishment ships and three civilian 'personnel and equipment transports' – steamed into San Carlos Water and began taking up their positions off the three assault beaches.

One older Type 12 frigate, HMS *Plymouth*, sailed into San Carlos Water with the amphibious force to provide naval gunfire support and close-in AAA defence while the six other escorts moved into a defensive array to protect the task group and its anchorage. Woodward's other 'County-class' destroyer, HMS *Antrim*, was designated the Local Air Defence Control Ship, and it took a central position in San Carlos Strait, while the Type 12 frigates *Argonaut* and *Yarmouth* were stationed in the north and south entrances to the Strait, respectively, primarily as ASW guards. Since *Antrim*'s Type 965 radar was almost completely blinded by the islands' rugged terrain sandwiching the warship, the Type 22 frigates *Brilliant* and *Broadsword* flanked the destroyer west and east, respectively, using their more effective Type 967 radars to look for high-speed targets through the 'ground clutter'. Meanwhile, the Type 21 frigate *Ardent* steamed south into Grantham Sound/Bahía Ruíz Puente to provide naval gunfire support for D Squadron, 22 SAS Regiment, in its attack on the Argentine garrison at Darwin/Goose Green.

Air cover was provided by TG 317.8's Sea Harriers, now reinforced to 25 – eight aircraft from newly formed 809 NAS had been shared between 800 and 801 NASs following their arrival in the South Atlantic as deck cargo on board the container ship (impressed as an aircraft transport) *Atlantic Conveyor* on 19 May. The SHARs had shared deck space on the vessel with six RAF Harrier GR 3s of No. 1(F) Sqn, these aircraft being delivered to TG 317.8 specifically to perform ground attack and close air support missions. Two CAP points were planned – one north of Pebble Island/Isla Borbón (W8 on the map) to guard the northern entrance to the Sound and the other towards the south entrance (W10) – guarding the expected approach paths. Recent losses convinced Admiral Woodward to keep his two aircraft carriers outside the 425-nm combat radius of the Super Étendard/Exocet threat, so the carriers were positioned 200nm to the east.

Beginning at 0630hrs, each carrier planned to launch a two-ship section every hour, *Hermes*'s 800 NAS manning the southern CAP, with *Invincible*'s 801 NAS pair staggering their departures by 30 minutes to man the northern one. This way, with only ten minutes 'on station time' available due to the half-hour travel time to get to and from their carriers, there would be one pair of SHARs in the Amphibious Operating Area about one-third of the time. Additionally, each ship had an 'alert pair' on deck, ready to scramble to replace those on station, to defend the carriers, or if an overwhelming number of attackers was detected inbound to the amphibious force.

CdoFAS finally learned of the British amphibious operation at about 0830hrs when a *Grupo 3 de Ataque* Pucará – one of eight scrambled from Goose Green airfield/

Dawn on 21 May 1982 revealed that TG 317.0 – the Royal Navy's amphibious task group – had arrived in San Carlos Water to repossess the Falkland Islands. (Tim Callaway Collection)

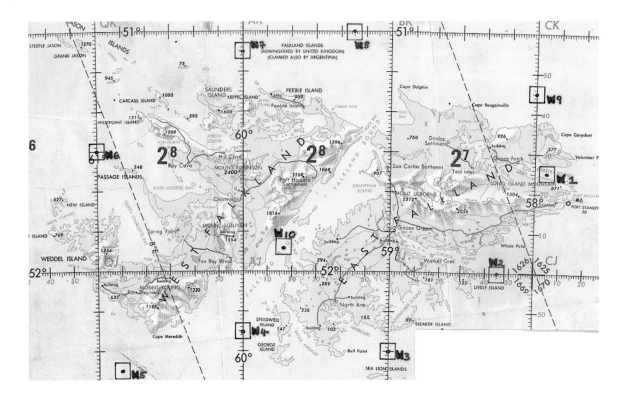

Sea Harrier CAP positions (squares marked with numbers prefixed with the letter W) around the Falkland Islands. The narrow stretch of water marked on the map as Falkland Sound is San Carlos Strait, where most of the first day's attacks occurred. (Tim Callaway Collection)

BAM Cóndor because of *Ardent*'s bombardment – spotted the ships in San Carlos Water unloading troops and equipment. Crespo immediately ordered the maritime attack plan put into action. Four waves of attackers were despatched, alternating Daggers and Skyhawks.

The first wave – 11 Daggers, with four Mirages flying feints at high altitude – departed their bases at 0954–1001hrs. None of the four fighter-bomber formations were intercepted by SHAR CAPs and all found their targets. *Antrim* was hit by one 'slick' Mk 17 1,000lb bomb (454kg) that careened through its Seaslug magazine, clipping two of the surface-to-air missiles, then smashed through a pyrotechnic locker before lodging in a lavatory, starting several small fires along the way. Its time of flight had been too short for the weapon to arm, however. The Daggers' strafing wounded seven sailors and knocked out the port Seacat SAM launcher. *Broadsword* was also heavily strafed – 14 men were wounded and two Lynx helicopters damaged. As the attackers turned to escape, Lt Pedro 'Caiman' Bean (in C-428) was shot down by a Sea Wolf SAM. He ejected, but did not survive.

Damage to *Antrim* was significant. The destroyer withdrew from the Strait into San Carlos Water, where its crew put out the fires and began emergency repairs while a bomb disposal party from *Fearless* started defusing the weapon. With *Antrim* out of action, *Brilliant*'s FDO attempted to vector the southern SHAR CAP against one of the egressing flights as they headed south down the western shore of East Falkland/Isla Soledad. From their orbit at 8,000ft, the SHAR pilots spotted the fleeing attackers and dived to engage, but the supersonic Daggers quickly outdistanced the SHARs and the AIM-9Ls shot at them.

The FAA's second wave consisted of 18 A-4s flying in four formations. One of them severely damaged *Argonaut* and another damaged *Ardent* as it was returning from Grantham Sound. A third formation failed to find their targets and another was intercepted by 800 NAS's Lt Cdr Mike Blisset (in XZ496) and Lt Cdr Neil Thomas (in XZ492), who shot down two A-4Cs between them – both pilots were killed.

By then it was realised that these warships were dangerously exposed to surprise low-level attacks, and that their radars and SAMs were largely ineffective. Considering that only one of the eight attacking formations had been engaged by his Sea Harriers, Woodward brought the carriers closer to the Amphibious Operating Area in order to increase the SHARs' 'on station time', and began launching three two-ships each hour in an effort to boost the vessels' fighter coverage.

Crespo's third wave consisted of ten Daggers, in three formations, followed by two formations of COAN A-4Q Skyhawks (*3era Escuadrilla de Caza y Ataque*). Hoping to overwhelm the task group's defences, the former took off in a tightly packed group – four Daggers ('Cueca' and 'Libra' sections) from BAN Río Grande and six ('Laucha' and 'Ratón' flights) from BAM San Julián, all departing at 1355–1400hrs.

The combined 'Cueca'/'Libra' flight arrived first, led by Capt Horacio 'Dardo' Mir González (in C-418). The formation had been detected at long range by *Brilliant*'s Type 967 radar before they began descending to low level, and the FDO vectored the 800 NAS CAP to an intercept point near Chartres Settlement on King George Bay. Lt Cdr Rod 'Fred' Frederiksen (in XZ455) led Sub-Lt Andy George (in ZA176) down through the weather and, underneath, spotted the four Daggers as they began accelerating at full military power to make their approach to the target area. With George following one nautical mile behind to look for escorts, Frederiksen unleashed an AIM-9L at the trailing Dagger. 'Libra 2' (C-409) absorbed the missile's impact and 1Lt Héctor 'Jote' Luna successfully ejected. Unaware of the SHARs, his comrades thought he had crashed into the rocky ground along their hazardous route.

SHAR XZ499 launches from *Hermes* to man CAPs guarding the amphibious task group, anchorage and landing beaches. The jet is flanked by two of No. 1(F) Sqn's six Harrier GR 3s, the latter aircraft being ready to provide close air support to the troops going ashore. Lt Dave Smith downed an A-4B with XZ499 on 8 June, the Skyhawk being destroyed by an AIM-9L.

The three surviving Daggers burst into Falkland Sound just north of Port Howard at 1435hrs to find the 3,250-ton *Ardent* returning to reinforce the warships defending San Carlos Water. Although the inbound attackers were spotted, the ship's Seacat 'refused to go', its 4.5in gun was masked by the ship's superstructure and its 20mm guns could not repel the Daggers' attack. From the bridge, Cdr Alan W. J. West watched as, 'the first aircraft released two bombs, one of which hit us near the stern and went off. There was an enormous bang, it felt as if someone had

got hold of the stern and was banging the ship up and down on the water. With the explosion, a column of flash and smoke went up about 100ft. I looked aft and saw the Seacat launcher about 20ft in the air where it had been blown, and pieces of metal flying in all directions.'

At 1445hrs, led by Román (in C-421), 'Laucha' flight ingressed unmolested, and raced into San Carlos Water to attack the two Type 22 frigates. Amidst a flurry of flying Seacat and Sea Wolf SAMs and chattering gunfire, Román and Maj Gustavo Luis 'Puma' Puga attacked *Brilliant* while 1Lt Mario 'Foca' Callejo took on *Broadsword*, all of them slinging BRP-250 parachute-retarded bombs at their targets. The SAMs – and the bombs – all missed their respective targets, but strafing damaged *Brilliant*, wounding four sailors and knocking out its Sea Wolf, Exocet and sonar systems.

Five minutes later 'Ratón' approached using 'Cueca's' ingress route through the valley between the north coast's Morandy Range and the Hornby Mountains. Now realising the northern over-water CAP was malpositioned, its pair of SHARs was moved to near the western end of this valley. These jets were flown by Ward (in ZA175) and Lt Steve Thomas (in ZA190). Because their Blue Fox radars were blinded with 'ground clutter' over land, they flew a 'Barrier CAP' – a racetrack orbit perpendicular across the anticipated ingress route – at 1,000ft, looking out the sides of their canopies for their approaching targets.

At 1450hrs, the three Daggers of 'Ratón' flight – led by Donadille (in C-403) – were approaching the eastern end of the valley in line-abreast formation at 500 knots and at an altitude of 100ft when Lt Jorge 'Daga' Senn (on the right side, flying C-407) spotted a SHAR ahead, high, flying south. The dark grey jet stood out against the light grey overcast, and he called out 'Sea Harriers at "three o'clock"!' Donadille later recounted, 'I turned my head, and to our right I could see the unmistakable silhouette of a Sea Harrier [in a turn] about 300m [985ft] above our flight. I had a strange feeling that his wingman was behind us. At almost the same moment the British pilot saw us and started a diving turn towards us. "Eject bombs and tanks, break right, go!" I ordered, and at the same time I did the same to engage the Sea Harrier head-on.'

Donadille's unsettling suspicions were correct – he and Senn saw Ward but not Thomas. The latter later recalled, 'I was about halfway round the turn when I did my reversal to briefly check my belly [outside the turn] and saw two Daggers in a close formation going underneath me very low and fast heading somewhere from Northeast to East. I was using a technique I [had] read in a book about [air combat in] Vietnam. [American pilots] were taught to look below every nine seconds when in racetrack course. "Sharkey" was at the South [end of our CAP] doing the same turn.'

Alerted by Thomas, Ward spotted the two Daggers and initiated a descending high-g turn to get behind Senn. Donadille countered with a hard turn to cut-off

One of the first to attack, Capt Raúl Díaz led 'Zorro' flight against HMS *Broadsword* on 21 May. All bombs missed but strafing wounded 14 sailors and damaged both Lynx helicopters seen on the stern of the ship. (Raúl Díaz)

Ward, firing his 30mm cannon. Ward tightened his turn to meet the Daggers head-on, Donadille executing another gun shot, but aiming was difficult due to the lack of tracers. Ward later wrote, 'I was lower than the leader and higher than the Number Two as they flashed past on each side of my cockpit. They were only about 50 yards apart and about 100ft above the deck. As I passed them I pulled hard to the right, slightly nose-high.'

Donadille and Senn's manoeuvring to the south countering Ward placed Thomas in an advantageous position. Thomas later stated, 'I barrelled in behind them, locked up a missile on the rear guy and fired. The Sidewinder hit the aircraft and took it apart. I didn't see it go in [crash]; I was busy trying to get the other one. He went into a climbing turn to starboard to try to get away. I locked up a Sidewinder and fired it. The missile followed him around the corner and went close over his port wing root. There was a bright orange flash close to the aircraft but it didn't blow up.'

Both Dagger pilots ejected and survived. Donadille later explained, 'I heard a small detonation, not very loud ... My aircraft went out of control, first pointing into the clouds above, then started a frightening pitching motion that flattened me against the seat ... Suddenly the Dagger started a series of fast rolls – parallel to the ground – and the control stick felt "soft". Due to the speed of the aircraft and the closeness to the ground ... I took hold and with both hands I pulled the lower ejection handle.'

While the two Daggers turned to face Ward, Maj Gustavo 'Grillo' Justo Piuma (in C-404) climbed and, after alerting Senn to the imminent danger on his tail, began a diving turn to make a slashing gun attack on Ward, and missed, passing underneath at 450 knots only 120ft above the ground. Ward recalled, 'Flashing underneath me and just to my right was the third Dagger. I broke right and down towards the aircraft's tail, acquired the jet exhaust with the Sidewinder, and released the missile. It reached its target in very quick

SHARs shot down one member of 'Cueca'/'Libra' flight, but the other three got through to put two 1,000lb bombs into HMS *Ardent*. One exploded in the stern, immobilising the warship – it was later destroyed by hits from COAN A-4Q Skyhawks and sank that evening. (HMS Ardent Association)

'Ratón' flight was intercepted by a section of two SHARs led by Lt Cdr Nigel 'Sharkey' Ward, CO of 801 NAS. (Nigel 'Sharkey' Ward)

Incredibly, although their Daggers were destroyed by Ward and Thomas, Senn, Donadille and Piuma survived the experience of getting shot down in combat. This photograph taken shortly after the war captures the only flight shot down by SHARs where all of the pilots survived.
(Guillermo Donadille)

time and the Dagger disappeared in a ball of flame.' Fortunately, Piuma also ejected safely.

The action of the day ended with 'Tabano' Flight – two three-ship formations of COAN A-4Q Skyhawks – attacking *Ardent*, mortally damaging the ship (22 sailors were killed and 37 wounded). West ordered his crew to abandon the doomed frigate, and six hours later it sank. During egress, the south CAP, flown by Lt Clive Morrell (in XZ457) and Flt Lt John Leeming (in XZ500) chased down the first formation, destroying all three A-4s and killing one of the pilots.

Of the six warships defending San Carlos Water, half of them had been severely damaged – one of them sinking – by the determined Argentine bombing attacks. At dusk the entire Task Group cloistered within the sheltering arms of San Carlos Water as the FAA's fourth wave – nine Skyhawks (*Grupo 4* and *5 de Caza*) in three formations – scoured Falkland Water for targets and found none. In the night the badly damaged destroyer *Antrim* escorted the three civilian transports out of the anchorage. The unexploded bomb in the stern of the destroyer had been defused and gently lowered to the bottom of the bay, but the kinetic damage caused by its impact had destroyed the ship's anti-aircraft capabilities. *Antrim* spent the rest of its deployment on ASW patrol and providing surface escort for auxiliaries in the Replenishment Area, before being relegated to stand watch at South Georgia.

Of the 12 Argentine formations that effectively engaged British forces, three were intercepted prior to their attacks – a 25 per cent mission effectiveness rating – two of which were destroyed or turned back. The Sea Harriers shot down four Daggers (a fifth was lost to a SAM) and five Skyhawks for no losses.

Weather precluded effective operations on 22 May, and that night the strafe-damaged *Brilliant* departed to rejoin Woodward's carrier task group, being replaced by the Type 21 frigate *Antelope*. The next morning found the British frigates forming a defensive circle in the widest part of San Carlos Water, with the LPDs, LSLs and replenishment ships anchored close inshore. Fear of an Exocet attack caused Woodward to withdraw westwards, and SHAR operations returned to the earlier pattern with curtailed 'on station' time. 800 NAS manned the Pebble Island/Isla Borbón CAP and 801 NAS covered the southwest approach to Falkland Sound.

Bad weather lingered, and the next day's first 18 sorties – six Daggers and 12 Skyhawks – aborted due to cloud cover or failure to rendezvous with their pathfinder Learjets or Hercules tankers. Finally, a flight of A-4Bs managed to overcome these difficulties and hit the newly arrived *Antelope* with two Mk 17 1,000lb bombs. One Skyhawk was lost in the attack, the pilot killed. *Antelope* later sank after the detonation of one of the two bombs.

Approaching from the southwest, one of the two Dagger sections from *Escuadrón III* was spotted by the 801 NAS CAP, who called out the inbound raiders and then dived after them. The Daggers were flying across the waves at incredible speeds and, even diving, the SHARs could not close to AIM-9L firing range. However, 'Daga' section could not find the targets tucked into San Carlos Water and escaped southwestwards.

'Puñal' section also crossed San Carlos Water without finding targets and, during its egress, Radar Malvinas detected the trailing 801 NAS SHARs and warned the leader, Maj Carlos 'Napo' Martinez (in C-429). The pair jettisoned their ordnance and external tanks and turned northwest, putting the Sea Harriers at 'deep six'. Once outside Falkland Sound, Martinez turned southwest across Pebble Island/Isla Borbón, his wingman, Lt Héctor Volponi (in C-437) following.

Alerted by the southwest CAP and *Broadsword*, the 800 NAS CAP sharpened their lookout and the wingman, Hale (in ZA194), spotted Martinez's speeding Dagger and immediately led Auld (in ZA177) down after it. Once again the subsonic SHARs could not close to AIM-9L parameters on the near-Mach targets. As Hale later related, 'It soon became clear that he was running out, going [at least] as fast as I was and I wasn't going to catch him. However, as I looked around, I caught sight of his No. 2 trailing by something like a mile and a half. He saw me at about the same time as I saw him – we were flying about three-quarters of a mile apart on a converging course. As he started to out-accelerate me, I just dropped in behind him and from about half a mile I got in a shot with my starboard missile. It homed in and went right up the jetpipe. There was a tremendous explosion and the aircraft disintegrated there and then. The wreckage fell on the west side of Horseshoe [Elephant] Bay.'

Volponi did not survive this engagement.

During the early hours of 24 May Type 21 frigate *Arrow* arrived in San Carlos Water to replace the sunken *Antelope*, escorting an RFA replenishment ship, an oiler and an LSL. By morning the four frigates were arranged with a pair guarding the entrance to the sound and the others positioned to protect the seven amphibious and four auxiliary ships from air attacks approaching from behind the Sussex Mountains, a ridgeline rising to 1,000ft elevation only one nautical mile south of the anchorage.

Additionally, because the frigates' radars were blinded by the island's encompassing terrain, Woodward despatched his best remaining Type 42 destroyer, *Coventry*, and the Type 22 frigate *Broadsword* to establish an advanced radar picket position about ten nautical miles northeast of Pebble Island/Isla Borbón. *Coventry's* Type 965 surveillance radar could detect inbound targets at long range and *Broadsword's* Type 967 search radar could 'see' low-flying 'fast movers' amidst the 'ground clutter' of the islands' terrain. Together they would be able to detect incoming raids and, unless the terrain masked their flightpaths, track them across the islands.

The previous days' operational tempo, as well as the mounting attrition, seriously impacted the FAA's sortie generation capability, so CdoFAS's operations order called for a single maximum effort that compressed five formations' 'time over target' to minimise the warships' ability to recover from one strike before having to deal with another. Twenty maritime strike sorties were launched during the day, ending with a Dagger three-ship directed to bomb British ground positions on the north side of San Carlos Sound.

Grupos 4 and *5 de Caza* launched 13 sorties against the enemy vessels anchored in San Carlos Water, targeting TG 317.0's LSLs and RFAs. They hit three LSLs, but lost one A-4C to the ships' withering AAA fire.

Between the two Skyhawk attacks 'Azul' flight arrived – four *Escuadrón III* Daggers from BAN Río Grande, led by Mir González (in C-436). The flight ingressed San Carlos Water from the south, 'hopping' over the Sussex Mountains, and accelerated to 550 knots in its descent towards the line of targets anchored along the western

shore. Mir González later related, 'We began our attack immediately – there was simply no time to discuss which target we would go for. Since there were so many ships packed together so closely, we could see the British had considerable difficulty firing at our aircraft, because their guns and missiles would have hit their own ships.'

As 'Azul' flight departed San Carlos Water westbound, Mir González continued, 'We were jumped by a Sea Harrier which sprayed cannon fire at No. 3 [Capt "Memphis" Maffeis] and No. 4 [Lt Juan "Pollo" Bernhardt] but without hitting them. We fled from the Sea Harrier and continued at low altitude for about 40 miles, then began climbing to return to base.'

LSL *Sir Lancelot* was struck by a Mk 17 bomb that came to rest in the ship's film store, starting a small fire, but like many of the FAA's unretarded weapons, the ultra-low level release did not give the fuse time to arm before impact. The ship was beached and evacuated and, after the bomb was rendered safe, it was under repair for the rest of the campaign. Rapier batteries claimed two Daggers destroyed and a Blowpipe team was credited with a 'probable', but 'Azul' flight's sudden appearance and high-speed attacks ensured their survival.

Not so fortunate was *Escuadrón II*'s 'Oro' flight, approaching from BAM San Julián, led by Díaz (in C-430). The 'Type 42/22 Combo' on picket duty detected the three Daggers as they approached the Jason Islands/Islas Sebaldes and the 800 NAS CAP, led by Auld (in XZ457), was immediately vectored west to intercept, descending to 200ft over the water and accelerating to 540 knots. As 'Oro' flight continued its southeast course towards Pebble Island/Isla Borbón, *Coventry*'s FDO provided bearing and range updates. Sufficiently offset to the north, Auld began a left turn to intercept, visually acquiring the speeding Daggers during the turn about five miles off the nose. Hauling his SHAR around in a tight, high-g turn, Auld arrived in AIM-9L parameters and fired his first missile at the left-hand Dagger. Even before it impacted he fired his second Sidewinder at the right-hand wingman.

'Oro 3' – Lt Carlos 'Perno' Castillo (in C-419) – was hit, the Dagger exploding and its flaming debris impacting the water, killing the pilot. From the right side, Puga (in

C-410) saw Castillo go down and immediately called out, 'No. 3 was shot down by a missile!' Díaz did not witness the loss of Castillo, but checking to his right he saw, '200m [655ft] behind [Oro 2] an intense light was approaching in a zigzag at very high speed. I realised it was a missile and that he had no time to react, so I shouted for him to eject. The missile entered his tailpipe and the explosion was so spectacular that it engulfed the plane up to about one meter [three feet] behind the cockpit. I jettisoned my drop tank and bombs, and entered a tight turn to the right to check out what was happening to Puga, who I was still yelling at to eject.'

Following Auld's intercepting turn in a fluid 'fighting wing' formation on the right side, wingman Flt Lt David A. B. Smith (in ZA193) witnessed his leader's missile firings and spotted 'Oro 1' ahead, out of range. But when Díaz went into his right-hand 'break turn', Smith closed and 'as my missile cross [on the HUD] flashed across his tail, the angry growl of "acquisition" pounded in my ears. A quick press of the lock button, and the missile locked and tracked – safety catch up and FIRE! A great flash and the Sidewinder leapt off the rail, homing straight at the target. Another flash and fireball. The Dagger broke up and impacted the ground in a huge burning inferno . . . In less than five seconds we had destroyed three enemy aircraft – but with no time to reflect.'

Díaz recalled, 'In the middle of my turn I felt a powerful judder in my aircraft, I lost control and immediately all the warning lights on the panel came on.' Díaz rolled out and ejected, landing injured on Pebble Island/Isla Borbón. Puga parachuted into the sea and, after eight hours in the frigid South Atlantic, drifted close enough to swim to shore. Four nights later both were flown back to the continent in a *Grupo 9 de Transporte* DHC-6 Twin Otter.

Encouraged by this success, the next day Woodward moved TG 317.8 to a position approximately 80nm northeast of East Falkland/Isla Soledad, escorting the civilian 'aircraft transport' *Atlantic Conveyor* with its precious cargo of RAF Chinook and Royal Navy Wessex helicopters that were needed to facilitate a rapid advance from the beachhead to Port Stanley. From this closer position, transit time for the SHARs was

Lt Dave Smith, in SHAR ZA193, prepares to launch from HMS *Hermes* on his historic sortie on 24 May 1982. This aircraft was subsequently lost on 28 May 1992 when its pilot, Flt Lt P. N. Wilson, suffered nozzle control problems during his approach to landing on board *Invincible* while the vessel was sailing off Cyprus. He ejected safely and the jet ditched into the Mediterranean.

PREVIOUS PAGE

At midday on 24 May 1982 two Sea Harriers, led by 800 Sqn CO Lt Cdr Andy Auld, performed a near-perfect radar-controlled intercept against an inbound flight of Dagger fighter-bombers. Auld and his wingman, Lt David Smith, shot down all three Daggers, killing Lt Carlos Castillo. The other two pilots ejected and survived. On CAP north of Falkland Sound's northern entrance, and controlled by the nearby Type 42 destroyer HMS *Coventry*, Auld and Smith were 'on station' for only a few minutes before 'Oro Flight', led by Capt Raúl Díaz, was detected 60nm to the west descending to low level. Auld and Smith were immediately vectored to the west and followed the controller's directions, accelerating to 540 knots while descending to about 400ft. At ten nautical miles they began a left turn to intercept the three Daggers, which were flying on a heading of 100° at 500 knots and 50ft. Auld called 'Tally' at five nautical miles and began a hard, left-hand turn to AIM-9L parameters. Lt Smith later recalled, 'I was in a fighting wing [formation] on his [Auld's] starboard echelon. He fired first at the left-hand [Dagger], flown by Lt Carlos Castillo. He then quickly shifted aim and released his second missile at "Oro 2", flown by Maj Puga. The leader, Capt Díaz, then went into a hard right turn, clearing his wing [jettisoning external stores] in the process, and was hit by my missile as he was turning through about south. I was visually tracking him as his burning aircraft descended towards the high ground [on the] south of Pebble Island ...
Moments before impact, I saw the ejection sequence begin, with the bullet pulling an orange parachute out of the cockpit.'

reduced to 20 minutes, increasing 'on station time' for the fleet's air defenders. Additionally, the *Coventry/Broadsword* 'Type 42/22 Combo' stayed 'on station' north of Pebble Island/Isla Borbón.

On the Argentine side, however, the high attrition suffered in the previous four days' anti-ship strikes drastically reduced CdoFAS's ability to continue the pace of its maritime air campaign. Each of the two Dagger squadrons was down to four serviceable jets, so on 25 May the only missions launched were sent to attack a suspected British radar installation on tiny Beauchene Island and possible ground positions on the southern tip of West Falkland/Gran Malvina. No targets were found.

Heavy attrition also affected FAA Skyhawk units, and quickly worsened. Eight A-4 sorties were launched in the morning and three of the attackers were shot down by naval SAMs – two of them by *Coventry/Broadsword*. However, the British warships' success doomed them. *Grupo 5 de Caza* launched six A-4Bs that afternoon, all specifically targeting the 'Type 42/22 Combo', and four of these sank *Coventry* and damaged *Broadsword*, without loss to themselves. While the 800 NAS CAP of Lt Cdr Neill Thomas and Lt Smith intercepted the Skyhawks, diving to accelerate to maximum speed and closing to three nautical miles astern, they were still outside AIM-9L launch parameters when directed to 'break off the chase' to prevent entering the warships' MEZ.

Finally, attempting to hit *Hermes*, two COAN Super Étendards put Exocet sea-skimming missiles into the *Atlantic Conveyor*. By frequent in-flight refuellings from FAA KC-130H tankers and flying a wide, circuitous routing totalling some 1,500nm, the two 'SUEs' outflanked the SHAR CAP west-northwest of the carrier task group. When they were detected at 1640hrs – just as they launched their two Exocets – *Hermes* and *Invincible* both scrambled their 'alert pairs', but these were 'then held to [the] North to prevent "Blue on Blue" [fratricide]' and never saw the attackers. The ensuing inferno destroyed *Atlantic Conveyor*, consuming three Chinook HC 1s (of No. 18 Sqn) and six Wessex HU 5s (of 848 NAS) onboard, and it finally sank on 30 May.

Following CdoFAS's five-day (21–25 May) maritime aerial campaign, FAA shifted its fighter-bomber missions to attacking ground targets as three of 3 Commando Brigade's battalions began advancing towards Port Stanley/Puerto Argentino (45 Commando and 3 Para) and Goose Green/Pradera del Ganso (2 Para). Minus their helicopter lift capability, which had been destroyed aboard *Atlantic Conveyor*, the troops' 'yomping' across the forbidding terrain consumed most of the next two weeks.

Meanwhile, southern Argentina and the islands were subjected to repeated blasts of dismal, drizzly, harsh Antarctic winter weather. Only a few armed reconnaissance missions were flown, and little was seen and nothing significant was bombed. The reprieve allowed *Grupo 6* to restore its strength somewhat, with *Escuadrón II* moving from BAM San Julián to BAM Río Gallegos with its eight remaining Daggers and *Escuadrón III* mechanics recovering their unit to the same number of serviceable fighter-bombers.

The only notable maritime strike mission during this period was on 30 May by the COAN Super Étendards. Believing that *Hermes* had been hit in the previous attack, the aim of this raid – which was accompanied by four *Grupo 4 de Caza* Skyhawks – was to hit *Invincible*. Once again, aerial refuelling enabled circuitous routing that outflanked the SHAR CAPs. The newly-arrived Type 42 'radar picket' destroyer *Exeter*

ENGAGING THE ENEMY

Once the SHAR pilot had successfully closed into weapons employment range and brought the target into the HUD field of view, he selected the appropriate weapon (AIM-9L or Guns) and manoeuvred to shooting parameters. In this case – using Lt David Smith's engagement with Capt Raúl Díaz ('Oro 1') on 24 May 1982, just off the northern coastline of Pebble Island/Isla Borbón, as an example – the pilot has completed a 'stern intercept' to about one nautical mile behind the target Dagger, which has gone into a high-g climbing turn, jettisoning his bombs and external fuel tanks.

The SHAR's flight parameters – 479 knots airspeed, turning through 120° heading and 360ft altitude – are presented along the bottom of the HUD. The radar is tracking the target and the AIM-9L 'missile head angles' diamond is over the Dagger's heat source. According to retired Cdr Mike 'Soapy' Watson, 'With the radar tracking the target, a "radar cross" was positioned in the HUD over the target. This was a hollow +, and, if you looked through it, the target is through

the centre – outstandingly useful. If you select the missile to "slave" it would follow radar angles both in azimuth and elevation. The "missile pointing" is indicated by a missile cross, which is a hollow X. So with the radar locked and missile selected to "slave" they should be in the same place. You would run in until you got a tone from the missile head. If you were happy with where the missile was pointing, you would press the "accept" button on the stick, at which time the missile would lock to the target. This would be indicated by the missile head "growl" changing to a chirping sound and the missile cross turning to a diamond over the heat source.'

From his engagement, David Smith recalled, 'The angry growl of "acquisition" pounded in my ears. A quick press of the "accept" button and the missile locked and tracked – safety catch up – and FIRE. A great flash and the Sidewinder leapt off the rails, homing on to the target.' Fortunately, Díaz was able to eject from the ensuing fireball and survived the engagement.

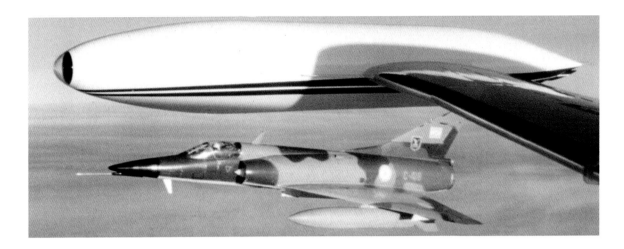

The long over-water distances from the two Dagger bases to the target area and the lack of in-flight refuelling capability meant that no time or fuel could be wasted in navigation errors. Hence, *Grupo 1 Fotográfico*'s Learjets, with their advanced and accurate navigation systems, were used to lead Dagger formations to and from the islands. (Juan Mothe)

detected the 'SUEs' by their Agave radar emissions and, according to the Royal Navy's official history, 'Two [801 NAS] SHARs were vectored out after them but . . . the Argentine pilots had a head start and were not in serious danger.' The follow-up A-4C attack lost two jets and pilots to the numerous SAMs and AAA fire.

Meanwhile, having eliminated the Argentine flanking position at Goose Green, the British advance continued slowly, ponderously, but irresistibly, closing with Menéndez's main line of defence. To turn the Argentine southern flank at Mount Harriet, the newly arrived 42 Commando (5 Brigade) was to be supported by two companies of Welsh Guards landed at Fitzroy Cove, on the southern shore of East Falkland/Isla Soledad, by LSLs *Sir Galahad* and *Sir Tristam*. Spotted by Argentine army OPs, these immediately became the targets for the CdoFAS's last maritime strike operation.

The day, 8 June, dawned clear and bright and Crespo ordered a combined Dagger/Skyhawk strike to neutralise the amphibious debarkation. Of eight *Grupo 5 de Caza* A-4Bs, three aborted due to refuelling difficulties, leaving five attackers, followed closely by five *Grupo 6*'s *Escuadrón III* Daggers, of six launched.

As the attackers approached the islands, *Plymouth*, an old Type 12 frigate with two single-barrel 20mm manually-aimed AAA guns and an optically-guided Seacat SAM, emerged from San Carlos Water to bombard an Argentine OP on Mt Rosalie with its dual 4.5in guns. Inside the anchorage, *Exeter* provided a SAM 'umbrella' over the frigate *Avenger*, two LPDs, two LSLs, an RFA oiler and a civilian transport. Additionally, *Exeter*'s FDO provided fighter coverage, controlling one SHAR CAP near San Carlos and a second just south of Fitzroy Cove. As before, the carriers' distance and other factors precluded the Sea Harriers from manning both CAPs continuously.

Exeter detected the A-4s as they began their descent from cruise altitude about 60nm west of West Falkland/Gran Malvina, but they were soon lost in the clutter of the island's terrain – *Plymouth* and the Fitzroy CAP were dutifully informed. Meanwhile, after the *Grupo 1 Fotográfico* Learjet pathfinder dropped the combined 'Perro'/'Gato' flights off about 120nm west-southwest of the islands, Capt Carlos 'Castor' Rohde (in C-415) led his three-ship directly to Cape Meredith/Cabo Belgrano, at the southern tip of West Falkland/Gran Malvina. His wingmen were 1Lts José Gabari Zocco and Jorge Ratti (in C-417 and C-401), while Capt Amílcar 'Mastin' Cimatti and Maj Carlos 'Napo' Martínez (in C-435 and C-418) were right behind them. Threading their way through and around low clouds, rain showers and snow squalls, the Daggers headed up the western edge of Falkland Sound. Having descended to low level twice as far out as the Skyhawks, they had approached entirely unseen.

As Rohde turned his formation east to cross Grantham Sound, intending to attack the LSLs in Fitzroy Cove from the west, looking to his left, at 'ten o'clock' (almost directly north) he spotted *Plymouth* alone and exposed in the middle of the waterway, initially headed west. Leaving the LSLs to the A-4Bs, Rohde turned his large formation around in a wide 270° left-hand turn and, spreading out to attack in line-astern, the first three Daggers came roaring in at wave-top height, with the second pair close behind.

The Daggers were spotted visually about two or three nautical miles to the south, and Capt David Pentreath immediately ordered the helm hard-over to return *Plymouth* to San Carlos Water as the raiders swung around and lined up for their attacks. Soon they were bearing down on the frigate from the port broadside and quarter at 575 knots. The attack was a typical Dagger weapons delivery – ultra-low altitude, extremely high speed, defying the optically guided GWS 20 Seacat and foiling the manually aimed port 20mm gun (the 4.5in guns could not be brought to bear in time). Martínez recalled, 'As we approached the ship her anti-aircraft fire came up towards us. We replied with our 30mm cannon but that was for psychological effect – the main thing was to get our bombs on the target.'

Of the nine bombs (one failed to release) dropped, *Plymouth* was hit by four, holing the hull and smokestack, destroying the Mark 10 ASW mortar and detonating a helicopter depth-charge that in turn started 'a serious fire'. Five sailors were wounded and the ship took a six-degree list as it continued into San Carlos Water, the *Avenger* quickly coming to its aid. As happened so often before, none of the bombs exploded in the ship – all of them passed through it.

Reacting to *Plymouth*'s initial air raid warning, *Exeter* vectored the 801 NAS CAP near Fitzroy towards San Carlos Strait, and the SHARs were soon in hot pursuit of the five fleeing Daggers. Martinez reported that '[Radar Malvinas] was showing the Sea Harriers ten kilometres [5.5nm] away, closing to intercept. We immediately pushed our speed to 600 knots to make it impossible for them to catch us. Because of cloud we climbed away individually, and rejoined formation at 35,000ft.'

While the SHARs were in a futile chase to the northwest, the five Skyhawks hit the two LSLs in Fitzroy Cove, setting both afire and killing 43 soldiers and seven sailors. *Sir Galahad* was completely destroyed by fire, while *Sir Tristram* was wrecked to the extent that it was useable only as a floating barracks. A follow-up strike by four more Skyhawks (from the same unit) sank a Landing Craft Utility (LCU), killing another five men. However, two 800 NAS SHARs extracted a harsh retribution, Flt Lt Dave Morgan (in ZA177) and Flt Lt David A. B. Smith (in XZ499) shooting down three A-4s between them – none of the Skyhawk pilots survived the encounter.

Fortunately for both sides, this was the last major air battle in the conflict.

Grupo 6 de Caza Daggers made the last strike of the war against Royal Navy warships, attacking HMS *Plymouth* in San Carlos Strait. Four bombs hit the frigate – none exploded, but one holed the hull, the subsequent flooding causing a six-degree list. Another bomb impact detonated a helicopter depth charge that started a serious fire astern and destroyed the ship's ASW mortar. (© Crown copyright. IWM FKD 191)

STATISTICS AND ANALYSIS

It is a fundamental tenet of air power that the attacking side should 'establish air superiority' in the battle area in order to enable other missions to be completed without interference from enemy fighters or interceptors. Correspondingly, the FAA's initial operations on 1 May 1982 attempted to do so. However, with one Mirage IIIEA and a Dagger being shot down by opposing SHARs in air-to-air combat, this proved unachievable without unacceptable losses. Instead, the FAA's fighter-bomber pilots had to rely on ingress profiles designed to stay beneath the ships' 'radar horizon' and use 'terrain masking' to neutralise the SHARs' ability to intercept them.

Subsequent operations on both sides were hampered by a lack of modern non-lethal capabilities. Because, until April 1982 the Argentine Navy jealously guarded its anti-ship role, the FAA was not permitted to have a maritime reconnaissance capability. Simply, it could not locate ships at sea, and had to wait until they moved inshore, near the islands, before any effective strikes could be launched. By the same token, the islands' terrain allowed the attackers to 'mask' themselves from ship-board radars until the last moments of their approach.

Likewise, the Royal Navy completely lacked an airborne early warning (AEW) system with a reliable over-land 'look down' detection capability, effectively blinding the fleet's air defence system to low altitude attackers until they emerged from below the 'radar horizon' or 'unmasked' from behind surrounding terrain. This made the SHARs almost totally dependent upon ship-board GCI for alerts of inbound targets and seriously limited their opportunities to intercept raids prior to the attackers delivering their ordnance.

During the conflict the FAA Daggers and A-4B/Cs, and COAN A-4Qs, launched 30 effective (did not abort due to weather, aircraft malfunction, navigation or refuelling problems) anti-ship strike missions, 24 of them during the critical five days – 21–25 May – encompassing CdoFAS's maritime air campaign against the amphibious task group. During this period, the command launched 180 anti-ship sorties, of which 117 were participants in these 24 effective missions. Of these 24 missions, SHARs engaged five (20.8 per cent effectiveness) during ingress, turning back two A-4 missions and completely destroying two three-ship Dagger flights – the fifth mission losing one Dagger but doing significant damage to *Ardent*. During intercepts prior to their anti-ship attacks, SHARs shot down seven Daggers and two Skyhawks without loss to themselves.

SHARs also intercepted two missions during egress, after bombs were delivered, shooting down one Dagger and three Skyhawks (three more A-4s were shot down during egress on 8 June). Frequently – during both ingress and egress – the chronically subsonic Sea Harrier, operating at low altitude where high velocities through thick air compressed the AIM-9L maximum employment range to about one nautical mile, could not catch their targets. This resulted in – during the attack approaches – them being 'called off' Argentine jets before entering the warships' missile and guns engagement zones or, during egress, their targets escaping completely.

Additionally, the lack of AEW support neutralised the SHARs' capabilities against a more modern threat such as COAN's Super Étendards. On all three occasions –

Five Dagger pilots lost their lives during the conflict, and three of them are seen here following the completion of their Dagger training at BAM Tandil. They are, from left to right, Pedro 'Caiman' Bean, Juan Domingo 'Pollo' Bernhardt and Héctor 'Lince' Volponi. The survivor, Comodoro (Ret-VGM) Gustavo 'Boxer' Aguirre Faget, still flies today. (Gustavo Aguirre Faget)

despite SHARs airborne and on CAP – these low altitude, Exocet-launching strikers were able to close with the task group and, in doing so, destroyed *Sheffield* and *Atlantic Conveyor* without being intercepted. As Ward wrote, 'The only means of preventing the Exocet threat were, firstly, to keep out of range and, secondly, if you had to come within the threat range, keep Sea Harrier CAPs airborne and transmitting on the Blue Fox radar. That way there was a chance of radar contact over a calm sea.'

Tragically for 32 British sailors, this chance proved to be negligible.

While the SHAR's operational and physical restrictions limited its success against high-speed, low altitude attackers, the Daggers and Skyhawks were also equally limited in their ability to cause more substantial damage to their targets. In their anti-ship attacks, Argentine fighter-bombers dropped 139 bombs (20 failed to release for various reasons) and scored 29 hits, sinking one destroyer, two frigates and an LCU and destroying two LSLs. *Grupo 6 de Caza* Daggers dropped 27 bombs and scored eight hits (29.6 per cent accuracy), damaging three frigates (one later sunk by A-4s) and one LSL. Considering that there was no peacetime training for FAA Dagger or Skyhawk pilots in anti-ship weapons deliveries, this compares favourably with COAN A-4Qs' 19.4 per cent accuracy (seven hits of 36 releases) – the naval aviators were trained in maritime strike.

The biggest problem – which is well known – is that only a third of the bombs (ten in total, one of which was dropped by Daggers) exploded upon impact with the target. This was the natural consequence of the Argentines' preference for survival over bomb effectiveness. In order to survive the modern Royal Navy warships' lethal SAM engagement envelopes, high-speed, low altitude deliveries were required. Nevertheless, one Dagger and six Skyhawks were lost to ships' SAMs and gunfire during their attacks.

Overall, the FAA lost two Mirage IIIEAs and 11 Daggers during the conflict. One Mirage was the victim of 'friendly fire', one Dagger was lost to a Sea Wolf SAM and another was downed by a shore-based Rapier SAM. The rest were lost to the lethal combination of the Sea Harrier and the Raytheon AIM-9L. Of 26 Sidewinders fired during the conflict, 22 were against Argentine fighters and fighter-bombers. Of these, four were fired out of range, one malfunctioned and one was defeated by a timely and effective IR missile defence (diving into cloud). The remaining 16 destroyed one Mirage IIIEA, nine Daggers and six Skyhawks. Almost all were fired from astern (AIM-9G parameters) and, for the Mirages and Daggers, the large SNECMA Atar 9C turbojet typically absorbed the blast – their Martin-Baker Mk 6 ejection seat worked successfully on the six occasions it was used.

One Mirage IIIEA and five Dagger pilots lost their lives in this campaign.

AFTERMATH

Following Menéndez's surrender to British ground forces on 14 June, the deployed FAA units began returning to their home bases. *Grupo 6 de Caza*'s *Escuadrón III* returned to Tandil on 19 June, with *Escuadrón II* following six days later. *Grupo 8 de Caza*'s Mirage IIIEAs flew back to BAM Moreno on 1 July.

During the war several Latin American countries supported Argentina with hardware, most notably Peru, which accelerated delivery of ten Mirage 5Ps that Argentina had purchased the year before. Following the conflict, work was resumed on Project SINT, the upgrade of Dagger avionics to IAI Kfir standards, now called 'Finger'. Using IAI and Thompson-CSF kits and Kfir noses, the 1987 upgrade included a HUD, the Elta EL2001B radar and indigenously developed software, all of which significantly increased the capabilities of the 21 surviving fighter-bombers. About the same time, the MGN-80 RWR system and chaff and flares were installed in the ten Mirage 5Ps, which became known as 'Maras' and were eventually reserialled in the C-6XX series,

'*Escuadrón 55*' was formed using some of the Mirage IIICJs acquired from Israel in December 1982. Commanded by Malvinas war veteran Maj Guillermo 'Poncho' Donadille, the unit was named in memory of the 55 FAA personnel killed during the conflict. Donadille is kneeling at the front, and fellow-veteran Jorge Senn stands on the far left. (Jorge Senn)

To replace Dagger losses, the FAA purchased 22 Mirage IIICJ/BJ 'Shahaks' ('Skyblazers', serialled C-701 to C-722) from the IDF/AF, the well-worn interceptors being transported from Israel to Argentina in three shipments, arriving in December 1982. (Guillermo Donadille)

with the last two digits being those of Daggers lost in the war. The Finger's last upgrade began in the early 2000s when GPS was integrated into the avionics.

To further replace Dagger losses, the FAA purchased 22 Mirage IIICJ/BJ 'Shahaks' ('Skyblazers', serialled C-701 to C-722) from the IDF/AF – additionally, two ex-*Armée de l'Air* Mirage IIIBE two-seaters (I-020 and I-021) were also acquired. Bearing Peruvian insignia for secrecy, the well-worn interceptors were transported from Israel to Argentina in three shipments, arriving in December 1982. Because they were considered operationally useless, the Cyrano Ibis radars were replaced with ELTA ranging radars and the jets' worn-out Atar 09Bs were removed and newer engines fitted in their place. After being thoroughly inspected, five of the Mirage IIICJs were used to establish *Escuadrón X* of the newly formed *Grupo 10 de Caza* at BAM Río Gallegos. When they were replaced by the upgraded 'Maras', the Mirage IIICJs became *IV Brigada Aérea*'s *Escuadrón I*, commanded by Donadille, now a major. The unit was called *'Escuadrón 55'* in memory of the 55 FAA personnel (31 pilots and 24 groundcrew) killed during the conflict.

On 17 March 1988 with the disbandment of the *VIII Brigada Aérea*, the FAA's Mirage force was consolidated in *VI Brigada Aérea/Grupo 6 de Caza* at BAM Tandil. *I Escuadrón de Caza-Bombardeo* operated the Mirage 5P 'Maras', *II Escuadrón de Caza-Bombardeo* flew the 'Finger IIIB' Daggers and the Mirage IIIEA/CJs were flown by *III Escuadrón de Caza-Interceptora*. Due to their low serviceability and advancing age, the Mirage IIICJs were retired in 1991. After more than 40 years of service the Argentine Mirages stopped flying in 2016, ending the 'supersonic age' of the FAA.

The SHAR did not outlive its former opponent. Learning from

Two years after the war, a pair of 800 NAS SHARs are welcomed aboard USS *Dwight D. Eisenhower* (CVN-69) during an exercise in the Atlantic. The SHARs' 'kill ratio' of 21:0 (fixed-wing aircraft) was the first time that any fighter type had inflicted losses without suffering any themselves – a feat unparalleled up to that point in aviation history. (US Navy)

the hard lessons of combat in the South Atlantic, the following year BAe proposed a significant upgrade that eliminated some of the more severe limitations of the V/STOL fighter. Most significant was the incorporation of the Ferranti ARI.50019 'Blue Vixen', an I-band pulse-Doppler radar with a detect range of 90nm against a high altitude, bomber-size target that also provided a multi-mode, look-down, multi-target capability. Futhermore, the aircraft was designed from the outset to employ the Hughes (now Raytheon) AIM-120 Advanced Medium Range Air-to-Air Missile. The upgrade also included BAe's new Sky Guardian 200 RWR, the AN/ALE-40 chaff and flares dispenser and the uprated 21,500lb-thrust Rolls-Royce Pegasus 11 Mk 106 engine.

The original 1988 contract provided for the conversion of 29 (later 33) FRS 1s to the new F/A 2 standard beginning three years later. The new SHAR (later redesignated FA 2) became operational with 801 NAS in October 1994 and fought in the Balkans, flying from *Invincible* and *Illustrious*. In February 2002 the MoD announced that the Sea Harrier would be retired from Royal Navy service, its roles being fulfilled by the combined RAF/Royal Navy Joint Harrier Force equipped with the upgraded GR 7A and, later, GR 9. One by one the three SHAR FA 2 squadrons were decommissioned, the last – 801 NAS – being disbanded on 29 March 2006.

Four years later, as a result of the British government's Strategic Defence and Security Review – a document disturbingly similar to the MoD's 1981 'Defence White Paper' that helped cause the South Atlantic conflict – the nation's whole Harrier force was suddenly and unceremoniously retired six years early so that its replacement, the Lockheed Martin F-35 Lightning II – could be funded.

The final iteration of the Sea Harrier was the FA 2, which was essentially an upgraded FRS 1 fitted with a Ferranti ARI.50019 'Blue Vixen' I-band pulse-Doppler radar, improved weaponry, better RWR and self-protection systems and an uprated Rolls-Royce Pegasus 11 Mk 106 engine. All surviving FRS 1s were rebuilt to FA 2 specification and 18 brand new airframes were also acquired. These two aircraft (rebuilt FRS 1 ZD610, in the foreground, and new-build ZH812 – the penultimate Sea Harrier), fitted with air-to-air refuelling probes, were serving with 801 NAS embarked in HMS *Illustrious* when photographed in 1999. (Tony Holmes Collection)

FURTHER READING

A number of good books have been written in English about the British side of the Falklands/Malvinas conflict, covering Royal Navy operations, ground operations ashore and air combat. However, most of these lack any more than the minimum account of Argentine actions required to place their narrative in context. A few notable exceptions attempt to provide information from both sides, albeit with a naturally British bias and frequently inserting supposition where historical facts are lacking. On air combat operations one of the best and more balanced accounts is *Air War South Atlantic* (Macmillan Publishing Company, 1983), written by Jeffery Ethell and Dr. Alfred Price. Published only a year after the conflict, it is remarkable for its comprehensive coverage and general accuracy, describing all aspects, from both sides, of aerial operations and combat in the South Atlantic conflict. However, it did inaccurately claim that, on 1 May 1982, Capt García Cuerva's Mirage IIIEA was damaged by an AIM-9L, directly leading to its loss. This mistake was repeated in many other books on the war over the years.

Much more comprehensive and in-depth – although repeating the same error – is *Falklands – The Air War* (Arms and Armour Press Ltd., 1986) written by Rodney A. Burden, Michael I. Draper, Douglas A. Rough, Colin R. Smith and David L. Wilton of the British Aviation Research Group. This is an expansive, voluminous and generally reliable book organised by aircraft types of both sides. Even better – especially from the Argentine side of the conflict – is Santiago Rivas's excellent *Wings of the Malvinas – The Argentine Air War over the Falklands* (Hikoki Publications, 2012) which is organised by Argentine air force, naval and army aviation units. Anyone wanting to know the details, and interested in personal accounts – from both sides – of those involved, should acquire this book.

For our purposes in presenting a balanced, though necessarily concise, account focusing narrowly on combat between Royal Navy Sea Harriers and Argentine

Mirage IIIEAs and Daggers, the co-authors of this book have also extensively consulted two Spanish-language sources – *Historia de la Fuerza Aérea Argentina – Tomo IV – Vol I* and *II* compiled by the Dirección de Estudios Históricos and *Dagger y Finger en Argentina* by Horacio J. Clariá, Javier A. Mosquera, Guillermo S. Posadas, Vladimiro Cettolo, Guillermo P. Gebel and Atilio E. Marino.

Other publications useful in writing this account were:

Briasco, Jesús, and Salvador Mafé Huertas, *Falklands, Witness of Battles* (Federico Domenech, S.A., 1985)

Brown, David, *The Royal Navy and the Falklands War* (Naval Institute Press, 1987)

Hobson, Chris, *Falklands Air War* (Midland Publishing, 2002)

Huertas, Salvador Mafé, *Dassault Mirage – the Combat Log* (Schiffer Publishing Ltd., 1996)

Hunter, Jamie, *Sea Harrier – The Last All-British Fighter* (Midland Publishing, 2005)

Morgan, David H. S., Lieutenant Commander, DSC, RN, *Hostile Skies – The Falklands Conflict through the Eyes of a Sea Harrier Pilot* (Weidenfeld & Nicolson, 2006)

Moro, Rubén O., *The History of the South Atlantic Conflict – The War for the Malvinas* (Praeger Publishers, 1989)

Ward, 'Sharkey', Commander, DSC, AFC, RN, *Sea Harrier over the Falklands – A Maverick at War* (Leo Cooper, 1992)

GLOSSARY

English/Spanish place-names in the Falkland Islands/Islas Malvinas

English	Spanish	English	Spanish
Beauchene Island	Isla Beauchene	Hornby Mountains	Montes Hornby
Bluff Cove	Bahía Agradable	Horseshoe Bay	Bahía Elefante Marino
Cape Bougainville	Cabo Bougainville	Jason Islands	Islas Sebaldes
Cape Carysfort	Cabo Corrientes	King George Bay	Bahía 9 de Julio
Cape Meredith	Cabo Belgrano	Lively Island	Isla Bougainville
Chartres Settlement	Poblado Chartres	Morandy Range	Montes Morandy
Choiseul Sound	Seno Choiseul	Pebble Island	Isla de Borbón
Darwin	Darwin	Port Howard	Puerto Howard
East Falkland	Isla Soledad	Port Stanley	Puerto Argentino
Falklands Sound	Estrecho de San Carlos	San Carlos Water	Bahía de San Carlos
Fitzroy Bay	Bahía Agradable	South Georgia	Georgias del Sur
Goose Green	Pradera del Ganso	Stanley Airfield	BAM Malvinas
Goose Green	BAM Cóndor	Sussex Mountains	Montes Sussex
Grantham Sound	Bahia de Ruíz Puente	West Falkland	Isla Gran Malvina

INDEX

References to illustrations are shown in **bold**.